Mixers, Signal Processors, Microphones,
and More

The S.M.A.R.T. guide to

Bill Gibson

THOMSON
™
COURSE TECHNOLOGY
Professional ■ Trade ■ Reference

The S.M.A.R.T. Guide to Mixers, Signal Processors, Microphones, and More
by Bill Gibson

System 5 MC cover image courtesy Euphonix (www.euphonix.com), LA-2A Leveling Amplifier cover image courtesy Universal Audio, Inc. (www.uaudio.com), C-12 VR cover image courtesy AKG Acoustics (www.akg.com)

SVP, Thomson Course Technology PTR: Andy Shafran
Publisher: Stacy L. Hiquet
Senior Marketing Manager: Sarah O'Donnell
Marketing Manager: Heather Hurley
Manager of Editorial Services: Heather Talbot
Executive Editor: Mike Lawson
Senior Editor: Mark Garvey
Associate Marketing Manager: Kristin Eisenzopf
Marketing Coordinator: Jordan Casey
PTR Editorial Services Coordinator: Elizabeth Furbish
Interior Layout Tech: Bill Gibson
Cover Designer: Stephen Ramirez
DVD Producer: Bill Gibson
Indexer: Katherine Stimson
Proofreader: Kim Benbow

ISBN: 1-59200-694-9
Library of Congress Catalog Card Number: 2004117622
Printed in Canada
04 05 06 07 08 TC 10 9 8 7 6 5 4 3 2 1

Thomson Course Technology PTR, a division of Thomson Course Technology
25 Thomson Place
Boston, MA 02210
http://www.courseptr.com

Dedication

This book is dedicated to my wife, Lynn, who loves bigger and cares more about people than anyone I've ever met. You inspire me to be a better man. I love you.

Acknowledgements

To all the folks who have helped support the development and integrity of these books. Thank you for your continued support and interest in providing great tools for us all to use.

Acoustic Sciences, Inc. Studio Traps
Gibson Guitars
Mackie
Mike Kay at Ted Brown Music, in Tacoma, WA
Monster Cable
MOTU
Radial Engineering
Shure
Spectrasonics
WAVES Plugins

About the Author

Bill Gibson, President of Northwest Music and Recording, has spent the last 25 years writing, recording, producing, and teaching music and has become well-known for his production, performance, and teaching skills. As an instructor at Green River College in Auburn, WA, holding various degrees in composition, arranging, education, and recording, he developed a practical and accessible teaching style which provided the basis for what was to come—15 books, a DVD, and a VHS video for MixBooks/ArtistPro along with a dozen online courses for members of ArtistPro.com. Gibson's writings are acclaimed for their straight-ahead and understandable explanations of recording concepts and applications.

Introduction

This is *The S.M.A.R.T. Guide to Mixers, Signal Processors, Microphones, and More.*
The title stands for Serious Music and Audio Recording Techniques and everything
contained in this series is designed to help you learn to capture seriously great sound and
music. These books are written by a producer/engineer with a degree in composition
and arranging, not in electronics. All explanations are straightforward and pragmatic.
If you're a regular person who loves music and wants to produce recordings that hold
their own in the market place, these books are definitely written just for you. If you're
a student of the recording process, the explanations contained in these books could
be some of the most enlightening and easy to understand that you'll find. In addition,
the audio and video examples on the accompanying DVD were produced in a direct
and simple manner. Each of these examples delivers content that's rich with meaning,
accessible, and very pertinent to the process of learning to record great music.

Table of Contents

Chapter 1 - Sound Theory

Chapter 2 - Interconnect Basics

Chapter 3 - The Mixer

Chapter 4 - Signal Path

Chapter 5 - Microphones: Our Primary Tools

Chapter 6 - Dynamics Processors

Chapter 7 - Effects Processors

Audio and Video Examples

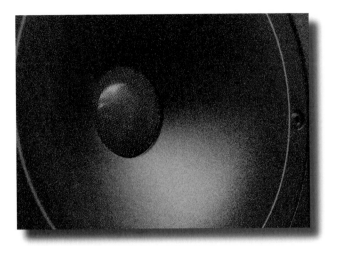

Preface

Welcome to the AudioMasters instructional series. By design, this book leads you through the essential ingredients in audio recording: core equipment, the building blocks of the entire technical and creative aspects of audio recording, and demonstrations that give you visual and aural instruction. Follow along on the accompanying DVD. Each audio and video example is clearly noted and is meant to be experienced in conjunction with the reading.

Although this work focuses on audio recording, the principles and procedures described often relate equally to live sound reinforcement. Audio recording utilizes some concepts that are not specifically incorporated in live sound, and there are some factors of live sound that are inconsequential in the recording studio. However, there is a fundamental core of theories and techniques that apply equally to both.

The audio arts, whether music, speech, sound design for visual arts, or archival are, on one hand, a beautiful art form and on the other hand a very demanding and meticulous technical undertaking. It's important that we are driven by creative motivation; it's also important that we expand our technical understanding to support and extend our creative vision.

Take advantage of the audio and video examples provided to add depth and clarification. These examples are produced in a simple, straightforward manner with a single goal—helping you understand the concepts contained in this book.

Audio Examples are indicated like this.

Video Examples are indicated like this.

The audio industry seems to change exponentially in this new millennium. The mixer I use in my project studio is capable of performing audio gymnastics that were not possible at any price 10 or 15 years ago. The fact is, relative to features, most computers today substantially outshine the most extravagant professional recording consoles of the '80s and early '90s; that's all within the computer itself without any mixer at all. Our creative options are enormous. We can bend, shape, mold, stretch, tune, distort, restore… the list goes on and on. With few exceptions, whatever you can imagine musically, you can achieve.

Technology has given us the ability to create in a new and exciting way. With that in mind, we all need to remain focused on what has drawn us to music and audio. Most of us just love music and appreciate a well-recorded, artistic, and emotional performance. That's the bottom line—capturing beautiful art. Beauty is in the eye—or in our case, the ear—of the beholder. I love the fact that each genre has a distinct personality. I also appreciate the fact that any given genre has the potential to thrill one group of people while repulsing another.

Yet, there is a common ground—appreciation of art. This universal appreciation, in its purist form, supersedes personal taste. In other words, good music is good music. Let your passion for great music and audio guide your attention to technical details.

This book teaches you specific concepts and techniques that will improve the overall quality of your audio recordings so that they will viably compete with music you hear on your favorite recordings. Herein are set out basic concepts and terms as they apply to our fundamental tools. Once you've grasped the principles and concepts I describe, you should immediately put them into practice. Each new concept or technique is mentioned to help you be more productive while supporting and enhancing your creative flow.

This material will help you get sounds that are competitive. Persevere! Keep fine-tuning your craft. If you're serious about audio as a career or if you're doing music just for the fun of it, this book is for you. The techniques described will help you make better use of your recording time. Your music will greatly benefit from your deeper understanding of the studio as a musical tool.

The primary tools of the musical trade, for both the professional and the amateur, are available everywhere, right off the shelf. Technology is more affordable now than ever before. With a mixer, some keyboards or guitars, a microphone and a computer, almost anyone can create a solid musical work that can either be completed at home, or can be polished off in a professional recording studio. With some motivation, imagination and education, you can (in your own hometown) make your music a financially, emotionally, and artistically profitable venture.

We're going to approach recording from a musical perspective. You'll study recording examples that fit real musical situations, and you'll learn solutions to common problems that will help you enhance your music. In doing so, you'll establish a base of knowledge. As your guide through this material, I'll keep the focus on details that make a difference in understanding how technology serves music, rather than how music serves technology. There are certainly plenty of places for a guy or gal who walks into a recording session with a voltmeter in one hand and an oscilloscope in the other—in fact they're essential. However, I tend to show up with a guitar in one hand and a mouse in the other.

A number of years ago the home studio was shunned by large commercial studios. In this day and age, it's a fact that very many commercially successful, major music projects are, at the very least, partially recorded in someone's home studio. Creativity has become the main issue. Whether you're in a large commercial facility or in a bedroom studio, keep your standards high and crank out the hits!

Sound Theory

The Source

It's very important that we understand the principles of sound in order to accurately capture music, speech, sound effects, or even noise. The sound source helps define the tools we should use to record it. Most of the time we strive to preconceive the sonic impact of the recording, imagining the sound that provides the desired musical or artistic result, and then go after it. Other times, we stumble across a sound that inspires a complete redirection of the artistic process. In either case, a thorough understanding of your recording tools is essential.

Any time you're recording an acoustic instrument, listen to the instrument first. Stand beside the musician and hear what he or she hears. Listen to the sound of the instrument, or voice, decaying in the room. Stand close and move away. Assess the sonic differences in the acoustic space. If you really want to capture the true essence of the sound, you'll need to make excellent decisions about where the instrument is placed in the room, what microphone you'll use, and where you'll place it in relation to the instrument. If you want to capture something other than the true sound of the instrument or voice, you'll need to be fully aware of the options available to you, and you'll need to be able to use them in a creative and artistically supportive manner.

The information we're about to cover is fundamental to the understanding of sound. Carefully study this material. It will help you make great recordings of great music.

Characteristics of Sound

Sound is energy that travels through air. Air molecules move in relation to the sound that moves them. When something vibrates, like a drum, string, vocal chord, etc., it affects the air around it. The air responds to the vibrations directly, contracting and expanding as the vibrating material completes its cycle of vibration. These vibrations cause continuous variations in the existing air pressure.

Sound Wave Reflections

Sound waves move in air like waves move in water. Interactions occur between waves and their reflections spherically in all directions from the sound source.

Video Example 1-1

Comparison of Wavelengths

Waves

Visualize sound in air like a wave in water. Any sound creates a disruption in the stillness of air, just like dropping a rock in a lake creates a disruption in the stillness of water. In fact, sound is referred to as sound waves because of this simple concept. As with so many concepts in art or science, the basic principles are easy to understand. Most complex theories and concepts can be stripped down to a fairly reasonable string of simple ingredients.

As you watch the waves in water travel, they minimize in size until they disappear, unless they reach an outer boundary, in which case they reflect back toward the center. The amount of reflection depends on the energy at the source and the distance to the boundary. As the waves

Acoustic Reflections Combine with the Source

Sound emanates omnidirectionally from the source. However, when we place a microphone in front a source we also get the reflections off each surrounding surface, combined together at the mic.

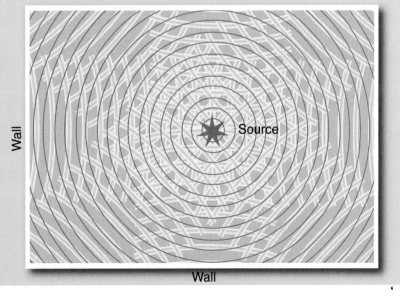

radiating from the source meet the waves rebounding from the boundary, it's easy to see the waves interacting and influencing each other's shape and size. That's exactly what happens to audio in an enclosed space. The reflections combine with the source audio, each influencing the other. This is the reason any given instrument or voice takes on a different character, or timbre, depending on the space it is in.

Our perception of sound is directly related to the waves in air. Consider that a lack of sound is completely still air—mighty difficult to find, but let's just imagine it for the sake of understanding. As soon as there is vibration by anything in the still air, waves begin. In relation to still air, each wave contains a crest and a trough.

When the wave touches our eardrum, the membrane vibrates in sympathy with the source, being pushed in by the crest and pulled out by the trough. This is explained by the principle of sympathetic vibration. When a sound wave strikes a body, which will naturally produce the same wave, the vibration of the body is called *sympathetic vibration*.

Crest and Trough

Audio waveforms consist of a series of crests and troughs that push and pull on the eardrum. This simplest waveform, called a sine wave, has the smoothest sound and the smoothest curve.

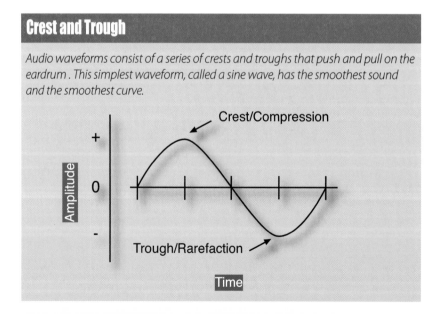

Push and Pull on the Eardrum

The pinna focuses sound toward the eardrum—it is fundamental in localization of sound. Compression and rarefaction are channeled into the ear canal where the changing air pressure vibrates the tympanic membrane, which begins the process of sending corresponding electrical impulses to the brain. Ah yes … the tree did fall.

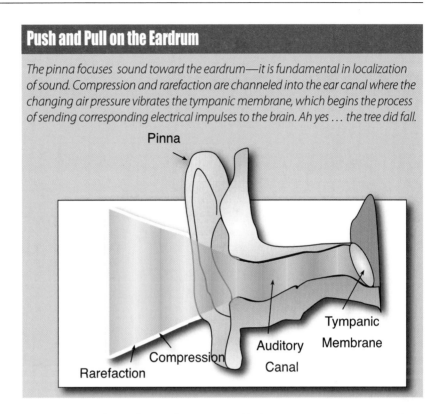

The simplest of sound waves is called a *sine* wave. When we chart the rise and fall of the crest and trough, the sine wave is perfectly smooth and provides an excellent illustration of the basic aspects of sound. To illustrate a sound wave we consider a straight line as still air. As the wave ascends above the line, creating a crest, our eardrum is pushed in—this is also called the *compression* portion of the cycle. As the wave descends below the line, creating a trough, the eardrum is pulled out—this is called *rarefaction*. Compression causes the air molecules to bunch together causing an increase in air pressure. Rarefaction is the result of the air molecules filling in behind the compression, resulting in a decrease in air pressure.

Keep in mind that individual air molecules don't travel from the sound source to the listener's eardrum. Sound is merely causing a chain reaction, which moves air molecules back and forth, causing the air

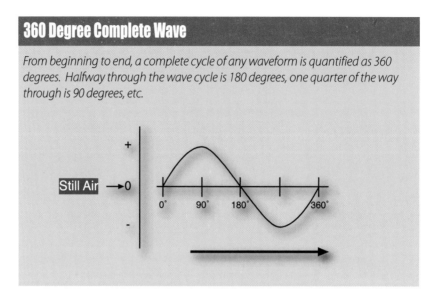

360 Degree Complete Wave

From beginning to end, a complete cycle of any waveform is quantified as 360 degrees. Halfway through the wave cycle is 180 degrees, one quarter of the way through is 90 degrees, etc.

molecules they're touching to move back and forth, and so on, until the air molecules that touch your ear drum initiate its movement. In Seattle, at the football games, we all get a big kick out of doing "The Wave" where a chain reaction flows all around the stadium. As soon as the person next to you stands up, you stand up, and as they're sitting down, you sit down. A huge wave moves all around the stadium, which looks really cool and for some strange reason makes you feel good about life. No one has to run around the stadium but the wave makes it all the way around. That's how sound transfers through air.

Speed

In normal atmospheric conditions sound transfers through air relatively slowly, at the rate of about 1120 feet per second (about 340 meters per second, 30 cm per millisecond, or just over one foot per millisecond.) Elevation, temperature and humidity affect the speed slightly. The speed of sound in air is determined by the conditions of the air, not on waveform characteristics like amplitude, frequency, or wavelength. There are plenty of formulas available on the Internet that take all factors into consideration for the speed of sound. For the purpose of our illustrations and calculations, 1120 ft./sec. will usually suffice.

Cycles

When a source has completed one crest and one trough it has completed one cycle. This represents a push and pull on the eardrum—one compression and one rarefaction of air molecules. We quantify position during the cycle in degrees. There are 360 degrees in one complete cycle. The zero degree mark denotes the beginning of compression (the crest): 360 degrees denotes the end of rarefaction (the trough). 180 degrees marks the mid point of the cycle, where the crest ends and the trough begins.

Frequency

The frequency of sound quantifies the number of times a wave completes its cycle in one second. In relation to pitch, higher frequencies complete more cycles each second. Frequency is expressed in Hertz (Hz) or cycles per second (cps). 100 Hertz, or 100 cps, represents a waveform that completes it's cycle 100 times each second. 1000 Hertz equals 1 kilohertz (kHz). As frequency increases, it's common to refer to decimal multiples of kilohertz. 2500 Hertz is typically referred to as 2.5 kHz; 5100 Hertz = 5.1 kHz. In common usage, we often refer to kilohertz simply as "k." For example it's common to say, "I boosted the vocal track at 4 k."

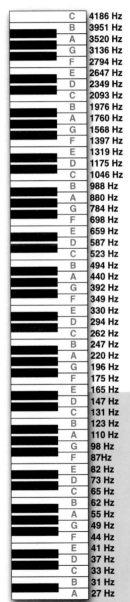

Frequencies Related to Pitch

Each musical note is related to a specific frequency. In the illustration to the left, we see whole number frequencies that, though they've been rounded off, indicate the way the frequency range of most music relates to pitch. The specified number of Hertz indicates the fundamental frequency—the sine wave that defines the specific pitch and octave.

The frequency response range of the human ear is roughly from 20 Hz to 20 kHz. Brand new ears, like those in a baby, tend to be able to hear frequencies above 20 kHz, sometimes approaching 23 kHz. Old tired ears, like those found in many musicians, probably don't hear high frequencies as well as they used to.

Pitch

An octave on the piano is the distance from a note to the next note of the same name. From middle C to the C above middle C is one octave. Mathematically, an octave above any pitch is twice the frequency of the pitch. On octave below any pitch is half the frequency of the original pitch.

Each pitch (note on a piano, guitar, trumpet, etc.) has a specified fundamental frequency within our system of tonality. We use a twelve tone system (12 notes per octave), tuned in a specific, tempered, way. There are many other tonalities throughout the world, utilizing differ-

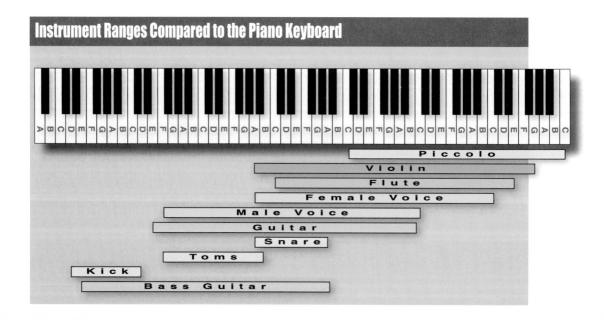

Instrument Ranges Compared to the Piano Keyboard

ent numbers of notes per octave.

Middle C on the piano has a fundamental frequency of 262 Hz. The A above middle C is often used as a standard tuning reference, and is called A 440—indicating a fundamental frequency of 440 Hz.

The frequency that defines the pitch name is called the fundamental frequency. In reality there is much more to a note than its fundamental frequency. Aspects of the sound wave called harmonics, overtones, and partials determine the individual character of a sound. The fundamental only determines the name and octave of a note.

As a point of reference, the lowest note on a standard 88-note piano keyboard has a fundamental frequency of 27 Hertz. The highest note on the piano has a fundamental frequency of 4,186 Hz.

Wavelength

Low frequencies have longer waveforms than high frequencies. The physical distance in air from the beginning of one cycle to the beginning of the next cycle is the length of the sound wave. The wavelength is often indicated by the Greek letter lambda. To calculate the wavelength (λ), we use a formula consisting of the frequency (f) specified in cycles/second, and the speed, or velocity, of sound specified in feet/second (v). Wavelength (λ)= Velocity (v) ÷ the frequency (f). $\lambda = v/f$

To calculate the length of a 1000 Hz tone, simply plug the variables and constants into the formula. The constant is the speed of sound (v), clocking in at 1120 feet/second. In this case the wavelength (λ) = 1120 (v) ÷ 1000 Hz Therefore, $\lambda = 1120/1000$ which equals 1.12 feet long.

The lowest note on the piano (27 Hz) is calculated $\lambda = 1120/27$. The result of this equation indicates a wavelength of about 41.5 feet. The highest note on the piano (4186 Hz) is calculated $\lambda = 1120/4186$. The result of this equation indicates a wavelength of just over three inches (.27 feet).

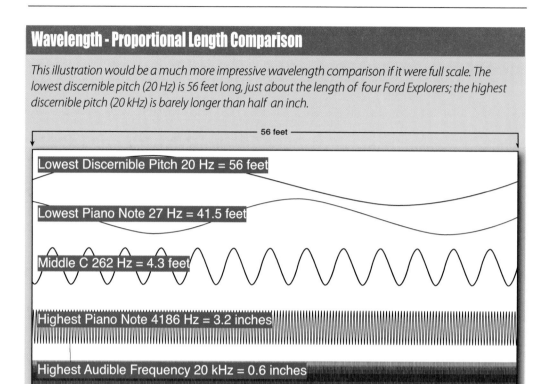

Wavelength - Proportional Length Comparison

This illustration would be a much more impressive wavelength comparison if it were full scale. The lowest discernible pitch (20 Hz) is 56 feet long, just about the length of four Ford Explorers; the highest discernible pitch (20 kHz) is barely longer than half an inch.

56 feet

Lowest Discernible Pitch 20 Hz = 56 feet

Lowest Piano Note 27 Hz = 41.5 feet

Middle C 262 Hz = 4.3 feet

Highest Piano Note 4186 Hz = 3.2 inches

Highest Audible Frequency 20 kHz = 0.6 inches

Our understanding of wavelength is crucial to our understanding of acoustics and how sound reacts to, and interacts with, its environment. There are some situations where we need to calculate the frequency of a specific wavelength. This is a simple task of cross-multiplication we find that $f=v/\lambda$. These equations will be important in our studies on basic acoustics.

Amplitude

Amplitude expresses the amount of energy in a specified sound wave. Charted on a graph, a waveform with twice the amplitude has a crest that rises twice as high and a trough that dips twice as low.

Amplitude only compares the energy of a sound wave. It's a simple comparison: a waveform with maximum amplitude that's 2.5 times higher than another waveform, contains 2.5 time the energy. The unit commonly used to quantify amplitude is dB SPL (decibels Sound Pressure Level). This is an objective scale based on mathematical logarithmic comparisons expressed as decibel=$10 \log_{10}(P1/P2)$.

Any increase in amplitude indicates an increase in volume. However, the correlation is not always direct—twice the amplitude does not always indicate twice the volume. The relation is dependent on the frequency and loudness.

Loudness

Loudness is a sound characteristic that involves the listener—it is a perceived characteristic that can be charted and averaged, but it's not simply a mathematical calculation. The common unit, used to quantify loudness, is the phon. Loudness is a subjective, perceptual aspect of sound.

The Loudness of Everyday Life

Examples of everyday noise levels in dB SPL

Weakest sound heard	*0 dB*
Normal conversation (3 - 5')	*60 - 70 dB*
Telephone dial tone	*80 dB*
City traffic (inside car)	*85 dB*
Train whistle at 500'	*90 dB*
Subway train at 200'	*95 dB*

Sustained exposure may result in hearing loss at these levels.

Possible hearing loss	*90 - 95 dB*
Power mower	*107 dB*
Power saw	*110 dB*
Pain begins	*125 dB*
Pneumatic riveter at 4'	*125 dB*
Jet engine at 100'	*140 dB*
Death of hearing tissue	*180 dB*
Loudest sound possible	*194 dB*

Government Regulations on Exposure to Loud Sounds

OSHA Daily Permissible Noise Level Exposure

The Occupational Safety and Health Administration (OSHA) is part of the U.S. Department of Labor. This organization has studied and prescribed maximum sound pressure levels in the workplace, in relation to the number of hours per day the worker is exposed. These guidelines are useful to help audio engineers guard against permanent hearing loss.

Hours per day	Sound level
8	90 dB
6	92 dB
4	95 dB
3	97 dB
2	100 dB
1.5	102 dB
1	105 dB
.5	110 dB
.25 or less	115 dB

The human ear is not equally sensitive to all frequencies. In fact, as amplitude varies so does the frequency response characteristic of the ear. The ear is most sensitive between 1 and 4 kHz. This frequency range just happens to contain the frequencies that give speech intelligibility, directional positioning, and understandability. Hmmm ... it's almost like it was designed that way. In fact, as the amplitude decreases, our ears become dramatically more sensitive in this frequency range.

So, yes, there is a difference between amplitude and volume. They are very similar at a certain point, though. Two scientists at Bell Laboratories in the 1933 charted a survey of perceived volume. They compared actual amplitude to perceived volume through out the audible frequency range (x-axis) and the accepted range of normal volume (y-axis).

The results of their survey involved generating pure tones through the audible frequency and volume spectrum at a specific amplitude, then asking numerous individuals to subjectively identify if the sound was louder or softer than the reference. Their survey, referred to as the

Fletcher-Munson Curve, is a very visual representation of why music sounds fuller at loud volumes and thinner at soft volumes.

Each curve on the graph represents perceived constant volume through out the audible frequency range. This, for example, shows us that in order to perceive 70 phons of loudness at 1000 Hz requires 70 dB SPL (amplitude). However, in order to perceive 70 phons at 50 Hertz, 80 dB SPL is required. At 10 kHz, to perceive 70 phons, a similar 10 dB SPL boost is required.

As dB SPL decreases the contrast becomes even more extreme between loudness and the actual amount of dB SPL required. At 20 phons, 20 dB SPL is equal to 20 phons. In contrast, at 50 Hz almost 65 dB SPL is required to maintain the perceived 20 phons.

Analysis of the Fletcher-Munson curve points us to the dB SPL range at which the human ear is most accurate throughout the audible frequency spectrum. Notice that between roughly 700 Hz and 1.5 kHz, phons are essentially equal to dB SPL at all volumes. Also, notice that at the center of the graph is where more often than not dB SPL is most similar to phons.

From this graph it is generally held that the most sensitive frequency range is from 1 – 4 kHz, although the graph might indicate an extension of that range from about 700 Hz to 6 kHz or so. Since this is a subjective study, some generalities apply but it is obvious where the consistencies and trends are.

For our recording purposes, it is constructive to find the flattest curves on the graph. A curve with less variation indicates a volume where the human ear's response most often matches loudness to dB SPL—the level where the most accurate assessments can be made regarding mix and tonal decisions.

The LOUDNESS button on your stereo is an example of compensation for the fact that it takes more high and low frequencies at a low volume to perceive equal loudness throughout the audible spectrum.

The most consistent monitor volume for our recording purpose is between 85 and 90 dB SPL, according to the Fletcher-Munson Curve. Notice on the graph that the 80 and 90 phons curves are the flattest, from 20 Hz to 20 kHz.

The Fletcher-Munson Curve of Equal Loudness

This graph plots results from a survey that relates amplitude (dB SPL) to perceived volume. This curve is valuable because it highlights the frequency response characteristic of the human ear. Since amplitude is a quantifiable energy level and loudness is a subjective characteristic, based on the listener's opinion, there's no better way to discover perceived volume than to ask human beings and then chart the results.

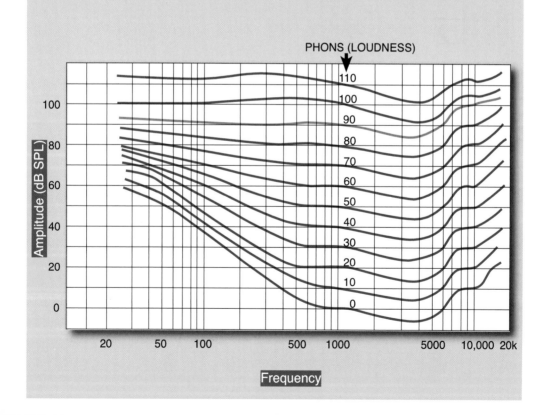

A, B, and C Weighting

Any piece of gear that quantifies amplitude must specify whether it's sensitive to a full or limited band-width. Weighting is the qualifier for sound pressure level measurements.

C weighting closely approximates full-bandwidth sensitivity. This is the scale that most accurately represents amplitude.

A weighting closely approximates loudness, attenuating the lower frequencies to resemble the response of the human ear (which is most sensitive to frequencies between 1000 and 4000 Hz.)

B weighting includes more of the mid frequencies in its sensitivity than A weighting. It's usually used in conjunction with A and C weighting in analysis of acoustical anomalies.

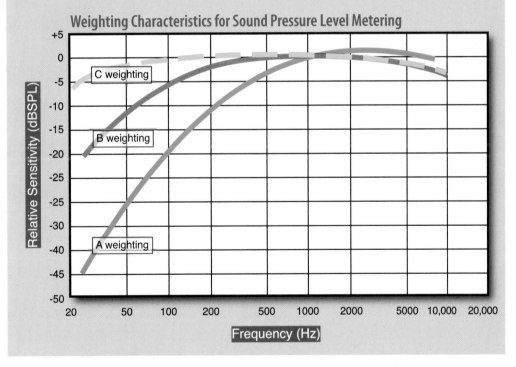

There are a few different devices available to help you quantify specifically how loud, in dB SPL, you have your system set. The simplest and least expensive way to assess dB SPL is with a handheld decibel meter. They are available at most home electronics stores and, depending on features and manufacturer, typically range in price from about $40 – $300. Most of these instruments offer A and C weighting, along with slow (average) and fast (peak) attack times.

C weighting is optimized for a full-bandwidth sources at levels exceeding 85 dB. A weighting filters out the high and low frequencies and is optimized for lower volumes. The A-weighted scale more closely reflects perceived volume, whereas the C-weighted scale measures amount of energy (amplitude).

Phase

We discovered previously that a sound wave is represented by one complete cycle—a crest and a trough—which is measured along the time line in degrees. The beginning of the crest is at zero degrees and the end of the trough is 360 degrees. The way multiple sound waves interact in the same acoustical or electrical space is called *phase*.

Since a sound wave has a crest, which pushes on your eardrum, and a trough, which pulls on your eardrum, it's fairly simple to visualize that if two identical waveforms happen simultaneously and follow the exact same path, their energy would increase as they worked together—in fact, they double in amplitude, meaning the peak is twice as high and the trough is twice as deep. As seen by your eardrum, the compression and rarefaction are doubled. Two identical waveforms, which start at the exact same point in time and follow the identical path through the crest and trough, are said to be *in phase*.

If two signals are out of phase, their waveforms are mirror images of each other. The electronic result of this combination is silence. When this happens electronically, the energies oppose each other completely—for each push there is an equal pull throughout all 360 degrees. Since we refer to a complete cycle as 360 degrees, we mark the center point of the cycle at 180 degrees. By delaying one of two identical waveforms so that the beginning of the trough of one coincides with the beginning of the crest on the other (180 degrees into the cycle), we create a scenario of complete phase cancellation. When this happens, we say the two waveforms are 180 degrees out of phase.

It's easy to create a scenario, electronically, where two waveforms combine 180 degrees out of phase. It rarely happens acoustically because of the predominance and complexity of reflections, along with the fact that we hear with two ears, which already receive the same waveform at slightly different points of time. Interactions between acoustic sound waves is, however, still an important factor in understanding music and recording. For our study of acoustics, it's most enlightening to recognize

Phase Relationship

Wave B is 180° out of phase with Wave A. The result of opposing crests and troughs is no air movement. No air movement means no sound

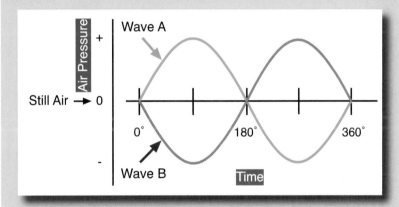

Conversely, two identical waveforms that start at exactly the same time (below) are in phase. They combine, resulting in twice as much energy.

The height of the waveform (the distance above and below the center line) is referred to as the amplitude. Amplitude corresponds to the amount of energy in the waveform.

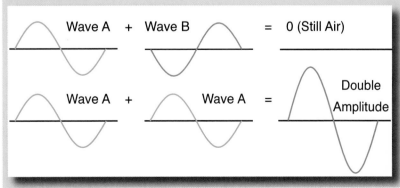

the concept that multiple sounds work together to form the whole.

Waveforms can combine out of phase at any point in the cycle. If two waveforms are 90 degrees out of phase, they interact together to change the resultant sound. Even though there isn't complete phase cancellation, we still experience the result of the opposing and summing forces.

There are a few different ways that negative phase interactions provide obstacles:

+ When multiple microphones are used in the same room, sounds can reach the different mics at different times and probably at different points in the cycle of the wave. They combine at the mic out of phase. That's why it's always best to use as few mics as possible on an instrument or group of instruments in the same. Fewer mics means fewer phase problems.

+ This theory also pertains to the way speakers operate. If two speakers are in phase and they both receive the identical waveform, both speaker cones move in and out at the same time. If two speakers are out of phase and if they both receive the identical waveform, one speaker cone moves in while the other speaker cone moves out. They don't work together. They fight each other, and the combined sound they produce is not reliable.

Harmonics, Overtones, and Partials

Harmonics are the parts of the instrument sound that adds unique character. Without the harmonic content, each instrument would pretty much sound the same, like a simple sine wave. The only real difference would be in the characteristic attack, decay, sustain and release of the individual instrument.

Since harmonics and overtones are so important to sonic character (vocal or instrumental), it's important to understand some basics about harmonics. As your experience level increases, this understanding will help you grasp many other aspects of music and recording.

When you hear middle C on a piano, you're hearing many different notes simultaneously that form together to make the sound of a piano. These different notes are called harmonics. Harmonics and overtones are a result of, among other considerations, vibration of the instrument; size of the instrument; acoustics; the type of material the instrument is made of; or the vibration of the string, membrane, reed, etc. Several factors add to the harmonic content, but it's a law of physics that harmonics combine with the fundamental wave to make a unique sound that is represented by one waveform. That waveform is a result of the combination of energies included in the fundamental frequency and all of the harmonics. The fundamental is the wave that defines the pitch of the sound wave.

The frequencies of the harmonics are simple to calculate. Harmonics are whole number–multiples of the fundamental frequency. In other words, if the fundamental has a frequency of 220 Hz (A below middle C), calculate the harmonics by multiplying 220 by 1, 2, 3, 4, 5, 6, and so on.

- 220 x 1 = the fundamental, the frequency that gives the note its name, the first harmonic
- 220 x 2 = 440 Hz, the second harmonic
- 220 x 3 = 660 Hz, the third harmonic
- 220 x 4 = 880 Hz, the fourth harmonic
- 220 x 5 = 1100 Hz, the fifth harmonic
- 220 x 6 = 1320 Hz, the sixth harmonic

It's traditional to primarily consider the sonic implications of the harmonics up to about 20 kHz, since that is the typical limitation of our ears and equipment. There is a controversy regarding the importance of the upper harmonics above 20 kHz. As we understand how frequencies interact, it's not difficult to imagine that the frequencies above our audible frequency spectrum have an affect on those we can hear.

Video Example 1-2

Harmonics - How They Combine to Create Tonal Character

Engineers involved in archiving music and sounds for future reference carry on spirited debates about this. High quality archival of important recordings is a big topic in the digital realm. Although digital storage seems very well suited to archiving because of its durability and long-lasting construction, the fact that CD quality audio (at 44.1 kHz sample rate) cuts off all frequencies above 20 kHz sheds a questionable light on its long-term viability for important audio archiving. Digital sample rates of 192 kHz or higher make more sense when considering the future of audio storage.

As the harmonics combine with the fundamental, summing and canceling occurs between the fundamental and its harmonics. This summing and canceling interaction is what shapes a new and different sounding waveform each time a new harmonic is added.

The terms harmonic and overtone are often used synonymously, but there is a difference. Whereas the harmonics are always calculated mathematically, as whole number multiples of the fundamental, overtones are referenced to intervals and don't always precisely fit the harmonic formula. In the case of the piano, for example, the overtones are very close to the mathematical harmonics, but some are slightly off.

Some percussion sounds contain a relative of harmonics and overtones called partials. Like overtones, partials aren't mathematically related to the fundamental in the same simple formula as harmonics,

Tone Interactions - Harmonics

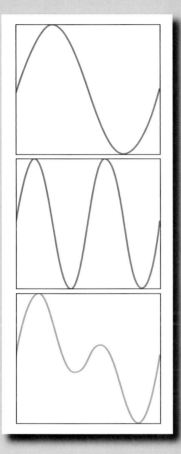

This is the fundamental sine wave. Its frequency determines the note name and pitch for the waveform that's built from it.

This is the second harmonic in relation to the fundamental above. It's frequency is two times the fundamental, so it completes its cycle twice in the same time period that the fundamental completes one cycle.

This is the result of combining the fundamental and the second harmonic. This new waveform has its own unique wave shape and sound. When waves combine, our ears no longer detect separate sound waves, they merely react to the one new wave that is influenced by all simultaneously occurring sounds.

and the effect that these sounds have can be very dramatic and interesting. Some bell-type sounds contain partials that are very far removed from the true harmonics (sometimes they even sound out of tune), but the overall sound still has a defined pitch with a unique tonal character. Partials can also be lower in pitch than the fundamental, whereas harmonics and overtones are considered to be above the fundamental. On bells, there's generally a strong partial at about half the frequency of the fundamental called the hum tone.

Harmonics, overtones and partials extend far beyond the high-frequency limitations of our ears. For example, when we hear the lowest piano note, we're really hearing the fundamental plus several harmonics working together to complete the piano sound. If we only consider that the piano contains fundamental pitches from 27.50 to 4186.01 Hz, it might not seem important to have a microphone that hears above 4186.01 Hz. However, if we understand that for each fundamental there are several harmonics, overtones or partials sounding simultaneously that go up to or above 20 kHz, we realize the importance of using equipment (mics, mixers, effects, and recorders) that accurately reproduces all of the frequencies in and/or above our hearing range. Also, if we see that the combination of these fundamentals and overtones is what shapes the individual waveform, it becomes evident that if we want to accurately record a particular waveform, we should use a microphone that hears all frequencies equally. If the mic adds to or subtracts from the frequency content of a sound, then the mic is really changing the shape of the waveform.

Shape

There are some traditional wave shapes that we refer to when describing sounds. Sine, sawtooth, square, and triangle waves each have distinct characteristic sounds. Sounding a lot like a flute, the sine wave has the simplest shape.

A sine wave is a smooth and continuous variation in energy throughout the wave cycle, steadily increasing in compression, then gently cresting over the peak to fall, smoothly, into rarefaction, then rising gently back to the center line. This simple waveform is also called a *pure tone*.

The fundamental is a sine wave, and each of the harmonics and overtones are also sine waves. When the fundamental combines with its harmonics to create a new and unique waveform, they create a *complex waveform*.

Wave Shapes

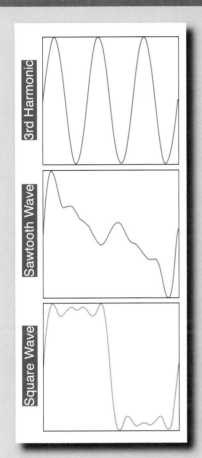

This is the third harmonic of the sine wave in the previous illustration. Notice that each harmonic is also a sine wave, but when they're combined with the fundamental and the other harmonics, an entirely new and unique waveform is created.

This is a sawtooth waveform. It's created by combining all harmonics in proper proportion. The sawtooth and triangle waveforms have a bright, edgy sound. Waveforms are given descriptive names based on the shape of their sound wave.

This is a square wave. It's created by combining the odd harmonics (1, 3, 5, 7, 9, etc.) in the proper proportion. A square wave sounds much like a clarinet.

It's important to realize that when we hear the fundamental and its harmonics, overtones, or partials, we don't hear any of the individual sine waves. Instead, we hear the result of the combination of all waves as one distinct waveform. The relative level of the harmonics determines their effect on the fundamental frequency, therefore, shaping and molding the waveform and creating a sonic character. This individuality or signature character of a sound, possibly called its color, or tone quality, is called the *timbre*.

Sawtooth, square, and triangle waves get their names from the overall shape of their unique wave. Sawtooth and triangle waves are edgy sounding and have more of a brass and bright string-type sound. A square wave sounds like a clarinet.

The complexity of the piano waveform is the result of a rich harmonic content. Piano is an instrument full of interesting harmonics. Listen carefully to a low note on the piano and notice the complexity of the sound of a single note. If you listen closely, you can isolate and hear several pitches occurring with the fundamental. We perceive the harmonic content, along with the fundamental as one sound. In actuality the single piano note is constructed of many sine waves combining to give the impression of a single note with a unique timbre.

The illustration on the following page has the fundamental wave drawn on top of the piano sound wave. This fundamental wave is very simple, yet the sound of the piano is very complex.

The Piano Wave Form

This is the actual waveform of a single piano note recorded in stereo. The top waveform is the signal from the mic placed over the low strings. The wave on the bottom is the signal from the mic placed over the high strings. Notice the complexity of these waveforms compared to the sine waves in the previous illustration.

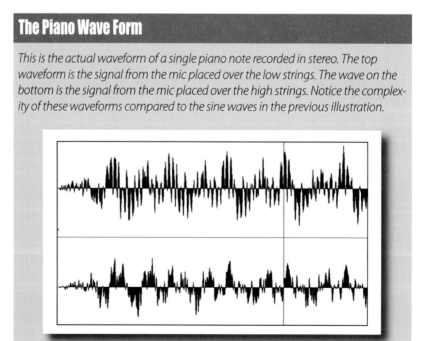

The Sine Wave versus the Piano Waveform

Notice the purple line drawn on top of the piano waveform. This line represents the fundamental frequency of the piano note. The fundamental frequency is really nothing more than a simple sine wave.

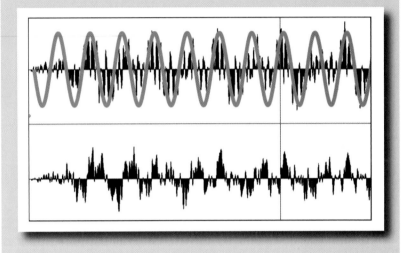

If you understand the theory of harmonics, you're well on your way to understanding the theory of sound. You'll also approach music and sound with a little more respect, finesse and insight.

Envelope

The envelope describes the initial action, development, and diminishing of a waveform over the course of time. There are four primary phases of the envelope of any waveform: attack, decay, sustain, and release.

Attack

The way a sound is initiated is called its *attack*. The attack phase sees the amplitude rise from zero to the attack peak. Sometimes the attack rises to exactly the level of the sustain phase; other times the attack contains a peak attack, called a transient, which falls slightly, after the initial attack, to enter the sustain phase. Most sounds with extreme attacks contain a transient, which exceeds the average level of the overall sound.

Examples of sounds with fast attack times are

+ Wood block
+ Slap
+ Snare drum
+ Acoustic guitar played with a pick

Examples of sounds with slow attack times are

+ A violin, gently starting a long tone
+ The swell of a Hammond B-3
+ The sound of a crash cymbal reversed
+ The approaching sound of a helicopter

The Envelope - ADSR

How sound develops, holds, and decays over time, comprises the envelope. The envelope parameters that we use to describe sound's amplitude characteristic over time are attack, decay, sustain, and release.

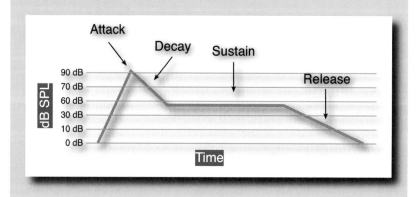

Decay

When the peak attack is reached, the energy might decrease quickly following the peak, or it could diminish slowly until it reached constant amplitude. The reaction of the amplitude after the attack is called *decay*.

Sustain

Once the sound has leveled from the attack and the decay, the period that the sound is still generating from the source is called *sustain*. Sustain is dependent on the generation of sound at the source. As long as the source continues, the waveform is sustaining. The sustain phase can remain at a constant amplitude, increase in amplitude, or decrease in amplitude.

Release

Once the source stops generating the sound, the envelope enters the *release* phase. The easiest example to explain the release phase is reverberation (natural or simulated). When a violinist stops and removes the bow, after a long, sustained note, the sound of the violin fading away in the concert hall represents the release.

Interconnect Basics

Basic Cabling Considerations

Wire is a very important factor in audio recording. There are several aspects of wire type and cable configuration that dramatically affect sound quality. For our audio recording purposes, it's important that we understand the physical differences between basic cable types and, in addition, that we experience and realize the sonic differences between a well-designed a sub-par audio cable.

Speaker Cables

Use the proper wire to connect your speakers to your power amp. Speaker wire is not the same as a guitar cable. Use designated speaker wire. Also, choosing wire that's too thick or too thin for your situation can cause a problem with the efficiency of your amp and speakers.

Ask a salesperson which wire gauge and type is best for your situation. Let him or her know how long a run it is from your power amp to your speakers, what kind of connectors your amp and speakers have, plus the brand of your amp and its power rating. If the salesperson gives you a glazed look when you recite all of these specifications, this indicates that they don't understand your situation. I suggest you get a second opinion.

Speaker wire must contain two identical wires, like lamp cord, as opposed to a line-level cable, which contains one, or two wires surrounded by a braided shield.

As a rule of thumb, a good quality 18-gauge speaker wire works well in most cases.

Line-Level Cables

Line-level cable is designed to carry signals like those from a keyboard or guitar to a mixer or instrument amplifier. Line-level cables also connect the mixer to the power amplifier or the powered monitors.

Microphone Cables

Microphone cables typically utilize two-conductor shielded cable with XLR connectors at each end. In the professional studio, microphone cables are often used to connect line-level devices, such as mixers, effects, and power amplifiers.

Devices that connect together microphone cables, at line level, use a balanced wiring scheme—devices that connect together, with regular guitar cables, use an unbalanced wiring scheme.

Some Cable Theory

An in-depth study of cable theory involves a lot of math, quantification of minuscule timing inconsistencies, and a pretty good grasp of quantum theory. However, basic understanding of a few concepts provides the foundation for good choices in cabling.

A cable recognizes a signal as voltage (electrical current). Small voltages travel down interconnecting cables (line-level, instrument, data) and relatively large voltages (currents) travel down speaker cables. A

Speaker Wire Gauges

Always use heavy-duty wire designed specifically for use with speakers. The chart below indicates suggested wire gauges for varying lengths.

The smaller the wire number, the thicker the wire. Thicker wire has less resistance to signal. To have minimal degradation of signal in longer runs, we use thicker wire.

Speaker wire often looks like the power cord on a standard lamp in your house. In fact, a heavy-duty 18-gauge lamp wire can work well as speaker cable in a pinch.

Whenever you're monitoring in stereo, be absolutely certain that the red post on the back of the power amp is connected to the red post on the back of both speakers and that black goes to black! If these are connected backwards on one of the two monitors, the speakers are said to be out of phase. When this happens, a sound wave that is sent simultaneously to both speakers (panned center) moves one speaker cone out while it moves the other speaker cone in. Speakers connected out of phase work against each other instead of with each other. What you hear from them is inaccurate and unpredictable, especially in the lower frequencies.

0'–25'	#18-gauge wire
25'–50'	#16-gauge wire
50'–100'	#14-gauge wire

magnetic field is created in and around a conductor as it passes electrical current. Any materials that optimize the accuracy of this conductance help the accuracy of the transfer process. Any design that takes into consideration the full bandwidth of audio signal relative to frequency, time, and content, becomes complex—more complex than simply connecting a copper wire between the output and input.

Once a few manufacturers addressed the effect of cable on sound, it became apparent to those who truly cared about the quality of their audio work that cable design makes a difference. Most inexpensive cables consist of a conductor that's made of copper strands and a braided shield to help diffuse interference. Not much consideration is given to bandwidth, relative to frequency-specific capacitance, and potential frequency-specific delay considerations.

Two main considerations must be addressed in cable design: balance of amplitude across the full audio bandwidth and the time delays as different frequencies transmit throughout the cable length.

Balance of Amplitude

Monster Cable addresses this with their Amplitude Balanced®Multiple Gauged Conductors. Since there are different depths of penetration into the conductor material by various frequency ranges, certain conductor sizes more accurately transmit specific frequencies. Therefore, it's implied that optimal conductance is accomplished by conductors that match the bandwidth penetration depth. With the frequency range divided among multiple types and sizes of wire, each frequency is carried in an optimized way.

Timing Considerations

High frequencies travel at a higher rate than low frequencies throughout the length of a conductor (wire). Low frequencies can't be sped up, but high frequencies can be slowed down by winding the high-frequency conductors to create inductance at those frequencies. When the windings cause the correct inductance at the specified frequency bands, all frequencies arrive at their destination in accurate and precise timing and phase relation. This corrected phase relationship restores the soundstage dimensionality, imaging, and depth. When the frequencies arrive out of phase, they exhibit time-domain distortions of phase coherence and transient clarity.

All the major cable manufacturers vary slightly in their opinion as to how best to handle audio transmission through a cable. However, there is agreement that cabling is a major consideration. As end users, it's our responsibility to listen to what they to say. It's our job to listen to the difference cable makes and determine the most appropriate cabling choices for our own situation. Not everyone can afford to outfit their entire system with the most expensive cable on the market—I realize that some have trouble justifying even one expensive cable. But the more serious your intent in regard to excellent audio, the more you should consider upgrading. Upgrade the cabling in your main monitoring and mixing areas. Procuring a couple of very high-quality cables to connect your mixer to your powered monitors is an excellent place to start. If you use a power amplifier, get the best cables you can afford from your mixer to the power amp and from the power amp to the speakers. It'll make a difference in what you hear, and therefore on all your EQ, panning, effects, and levels.

Do Cables Really Sound Different?

The difference between the sound of a poorly designed and a brilliantly designed cable is extreme in most cases. If a narrow bandwidth signal comprised of mid frequencies and few transients is compared on two vastly different cables, the audible differences might be minimal. However, when full-bandwidth audio, rich in transient content, dimensionality, and depth, is compared between a marginal and an excellent cable, there will typically be a dramatic and noticeable difference in sound quality.

Listen for yourself. Most pro audio dealers are happy to show off their higher-priced product. When comparing equipment, it's usually best to use high-quality audio that receives industry praise for its excellence. After all, that's the standard you are trying to meet or beat.

Young recordists are usually happy to get a system connected any way it'll work. To dwell on whether or not the cable is making any difference somehow falls near the bottom of the list of priorities. However, once the rest of the details fall into place and there's a little space for further optimizing, cable comparison might come to mind. In the meantime, we wonder why we can't quite get the acoustic guitar to sound full with smooth transients. We wonder why our mixes sound a little thick when we play them back on a better system, and we wonder why our vocal sound never seems as clear as our favorite recordings. It's tempting, though not productive, to save a few dollars on cable while we make sure our mixer and effects are the newest and coolest on the block. Cable quality is a core consideration. It's worthwhile to implement high-quality cable as soon as possible.

In reality, we'd be better off to build a system out of fewer components connected together with excellent cable. There are several very good cable manufacturers. Check with your local dealer to find out who's making great cable. It's not cheap, but it affects everything you do. If the cables that connect your mixer to your powered monitors are marginal in quality, you'll base every decision concerning the sound of your music on a false premise.

Listen to Audio Example 2-1. The acoustic guitar is first miked and recorded through some common quality cable. Then it's recorded through a microphone with some very high quality Monster Cable. Notice the difference in transient sounds, depth, and transparency.

Audio Example 2-1

Mic on Acoustic Guitar Using Common Mic Cable then Monster Studio Pro 1000 Cable

Audio Example 2-2 demonstrates the difference in vocal sound using marginal mic cable first, then a high-quality mic cable from Monster Cable. Notice the difference in transient sounds, depth, and transparency.

Audio Example 2-2

Vocal Using Common Mic Cable then Monster Studio Pro 1000 Cable

The previous examples demonstrate the difference cable choice makes on individual instrument tracks. These differences are magnified in the mastering process when the entire mix is conducted from the source to the final replication master. In mastering, wherever signal passes through cable, get the best possible cable for the job.

Digital-Interconnect Cables

Digital-interconnect cables also have an effect on the sound quality of digital masters and clones. Listen to Audio Examples 4 through 8. In each example a different cable and format configuration is demonstrated.

Listen specifically to all frequency ranges as well as transients. Also, consider the "feel" of the recording. Often, the factor that makes one setup sound better than another is difficult to explain, but it's easy to feel. The following examples use exactly the same program material as well as the identical transfer process to the included CD.

The differences you hear on your setup depend greatly on the quality and accuracy of your monitoring system as well as your insight and perception. Once you understand and experience subtle sonic differences you'll realize the powerful impact they hold for your musical expression. Constantly compare and analyze the details of your music. It will result in much more competitive quality. You'll realize more satisfaction and you'll probably get more work.

Audio Example 2-3

AES/EBU to DAT Using Common Cable then SP1000 AES Silver Digital Monster Cable

Audio Example 2-4

S/P DIF to DAT Using Common RCA Cables then M1000 D Silver Digital Monster Cable

Audio Example 2-5

Analog Out to DAT Using Common XLR Cables then Prolink Studio Pro 1000 XLR Monster Cables

Audio Example 2-6

ADAT Light Pipe into Digital Performer Using Common Optical Cable, Bounced to Disk

Audio Example 2-7

ADAT Light Pipe into Digital Performer Using Monster Cable's Interlink Digital Light Speed 100 Optical Cable, Bounced to Disk

If you can't hear much difference on some of these comparisons, try listening on different systems. Try auditioning several different monitors, power amps, or mixers with your own system. Keep in mind that there is a substantial cost difference between cables. It's entirely possible to spend more on the cable connecting two devices than you spend on either device, or maybe both devices. Cable prices vary greatly. With a budget in mind, choose to connect your basic ingredients with the best cable possible.

Cable differences, in many cases, make a huge impact on the sonic character and quality of a recording. In fact, whether digital or analog cables are tested, the differences are often so extreme that they can be seen in the onscreen waveforms of your digital audio workstation. Try this test for yourself.

Impedance

It's my intent here to add a little depth to your understanding of two topics: high versus low impedance and balanced versus unbalanced wiring schemes. This explanation will not be so technically in-depth that only those on a higher mental plane will dare to read it. It's a simple, albeit fairly thorough, peek at two very important factors in the recording equation.

Impedance is the resistance to the flow of electrical current. High impedance is high resistance to the flow of electrical current; low impedance is low resistance to the flow of electrical current. If you keep that simple mental picture in mind, the rest of the details should fall into place nicely.

Basic Terminology

Ohm (indicated by Greek letter, omega (Ω): An ohm is the unit of resistance to the flow of electrical current used to measure impedance

Impedance: Resistance to the flow of electrical current

Z: The abbreviation and symbol used in place of the word impedance

Hi Z: High impedance. The exact numerical tag (in Ω) for high impedance varies, depending on whether we're dealing with input impedance or output impedance. It's generally in the range of 5,000 – 15,000 Ω for output impedance and 50,000 Ω to 1,000,000 Ω for input impedance. It's important here to understand that hi Z is usually greater than 5,000 – 10,000 Ω.

Lo Z: Low impedance. The exact numerical tag (in Ω) varies for low impedance as well as high impedance. It's generally in the range of 50 – 300 Ω for output impedance. It's normal for microphone output impedance to be between 50 and 150 Ω and 500 – 3000 Ω for input impedance. Normal input impedance for lo Z mixers is 600 Ω. Essentially, lo Z usually uses small numbers below 600 Ω.

Output impedance: The actual impedance (resistance to the electron flow measured in Ω) at the output of a device (microphone, amplifier, guitar, keyboard). To keep it simple, realize that the output impedance is designed to work well with specific input impedance.

Input impedance: The actual impedance (resistance to the electron flow measured in Ω) at the input of a device. To keep it simple, realize that the input impedance is designed to work well with specific output impedance. Low impedance and high impedance are not compatible.

Compatibility Between Hi Z and Lo Z

The reason lo and hi Z don't work together is really pretty simple. The most common analogy for explaining the incompatibility between low impedance and high impedance involves a couple of simple water pipes and some water. In this analogy, water represents electricity and the size of the pipe represents the amount of impedance (Z).

Imagine a very small pipe. The small pipe represents hi Z because no matter how much water (electrical current) is at the entrance (input) of the small pipe, only a limited amount of water can get through the pipe at once. Its physical size limits the amount of water that can pass through the pipe in a period of time.

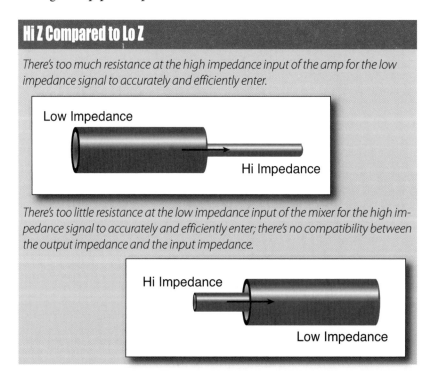

Hi Z Compared to Lo Z

There's too much resistance at the high impedance input of the amp for the low impedance signal to accurately and efficiently enter.

Low Impedance

Hi Impedance

There's too little resistance at the low impedance input of the mixer for the high impedance signal to accurately and efficiently enter; there's no compatibility between the output impedance and the input impedance.

Hi Impedance

Low Impedance

If you plug the output of a low-impedance mic into the input of a high-impedance amplifier, you have a problem. Imagine the microphone signal traveling through a very large pipe (lo Z). It's expecting to see a similar sized pipe at the input of a low-impedance amplifier. When it meets the small pipe (hi Z) at the input of the hi Z amplifier, it's impossible for the complete low-impedance signal to efficiently and accurately enter the small pipe. There's too much resistance to the signal flow; the pipe's too small.

This analogy is very appropriate because the result of plugging the output of a lo Z mic into the input of a hi Z amp is insufficient level. The amp might be turned up to maximum, but you'll barely be able to hear the signal from the mic; there's too much resistance at the amplifier input.

Compatible Impedance

This arrangement is in accordance with the design concept: a hi Z output feeding into a hi Z input. Notice that the pipes aren't identical in size. This is part of the design and is what you'll find in real life use—both pipes are small, representing hi Z.

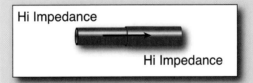

Hi Impedance

Hi Impedance

There's too little resistance at the low impedance input of the mixer for the high impedance signal to accurately and efficiently enter; there's no compatibility between the output impedance and the input impedance.

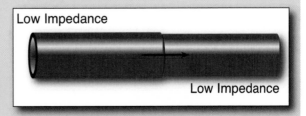

Low Impedance

Low Impedance

The other incompatible scenario involves attempting to plug a high-impedance output (microphone, guitar, keyboard, etc.) into a low-impedance input (mixer, amp, speaker, etc.). In this case, the hi Z output (small pipe) is expecting to meet a hi Z input (small pipe); in other words, it's expecting to meet high resistance. If the high-impedance output signal is plugged into a low-impedance input, the signal meets practically no resistance and therefore almost immediately overdrives the input.

Practically speaking, when you plug a high-impedance guitar output into a lo Z mixer input, the input level can hardly be turned up before

Line Cables (Musical Instrument Cables)

This illustration shows the construction of typical wire used for unbalanced cables. Notice that the hot lead is stranded wire in the center core; the shield is braided wire isolated from the hot lead by a plastic tube; and around the shield is a plastic or rubber insulating material.

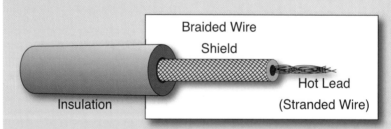

The illustration below shows the parts of a typical 1/4" line cable. The tip carries the actual musical signal. The sleeve is connected to the shield which is designed to absorb, diffuse and reject interference. The other common unbalanced connector is the RCA phono plug.

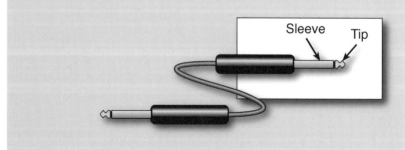

the VU meters read 0 VU; even then, the sound you hear is usually distorted because there's not enough resistance at the input.

High-impedance outputs are supposed to meet high-impedance inputs; low-impedance outputs are supposed to meet low-impedance inputs. It's not true that the input and output impedance need to be identical. In fact, the input impedance is generally supposed to be about ten times the output impedance, but as I mentioned earlier, we need to keep in mind that high impedance uses high ratings (above 10,000 Ω) and low impedance uses low ratings (typically below 1000 Ω).

Audio Example 2-8

High Impedance Instrument into a Low Impedance Input

Audio Example 2-9

Low impedance Mic into a High Impedance Input

We can simply use an impedance transformer—also called a line matching transformer or direct box—to change impedance from high to low or low to high; that's the easy part. We should, however, strive for a thorough understanding of why we do what we do. This simple explanation of impedance is meant to get you started toward your enlightenment. It is admittedly primary in its depth, but it functions as an excellent point of reference for further technical growth.

Balanced versus Unbalanced

For the purposes of this course, we'll cover this topic—much like we did with impedance—using simple visual references and non-technical language. Some of the basic differences between balanced and unbalanced wiring schemes are simple, and some of the technical differences are brilliant; let's look at these two types of wiring.

As a point of reference remember this: Almost all guitars are unbalanced and almost all low-impedance mics are balanced. If we dissect the cables that connect the guitar to the amp or the mic to the mixer, we'll learn a lot about the concept of balanced and unbalanced wiring.

Basic Terminology

Lead (pronounced, leed): Another term for wire.

Hot lead: In a cable, the hot lead is the wire carrying the desired sound or signal. From a guitar, the hot lead carries the guitar signal from the magnetic pickup to the input of the amplifier.

Braided shield: Cables for instruments, mics and outboard gear—pretty much anything other than speaker cable—have one or two wires, or hot leads, carrying the desired signal. Surrounding the hot leads are very thin strands of wire braided into a tube so that electrostatic noises and interferences can be diffused, absorbed and rejected. This braided tube that surrounds the hot leads is called the shield.

Unbalanced Guitar Cables

Normal guitar and keyboard cables, also called line cables, contain one hot lead to carry the instrument signal; the hot lead is surrounded by a braided wire shield. The purpose of the shield is to diffuse, absorb, and reject electrostatic noises and interference.

This system works pretty well within its limitations. Radio signals and other interference is kept from reaching the hot lead by the braided shield—as long as the cable is shorter than about 20 feet. Once the cable is longer than 20 feet, there's so much interference bombarding the shield that the hot lead starts to carry the interference along with the musical signal. The long cable is acting as a crude antenna and is picking up plenty of transmissions from multiple transmitters. This fact is true even when we study balanced cables; the main difference is that the balanced wiring scheme cleverly beats the system by using the system.

Wire for Balanced Cables (2-conductor Shielded)

Most wire for balanced cables has two separate leads twisted together in the center core throughout the length of the cable. Both of these leads carry the signal and connect to pins two and three; the braided shield connects to ground.

The wire connected to pin two is typically called the hot lead because it carries the signal. The wire connected to pin 3, referred to as neutral, also carries the signal although it's 180 degrees out of phase with pin two, throughout the length of the cable.

Twisted pair carrying the signal—hot (+) and neutral (−)

Three-Point Connectors

Any three-point connector can be used on balanced cables. As long as there's a place for the two hot leads and a ground to connect, the system will work. XLR connectors are the most common, but the quarter inch tip-ring-sleeve plug—like the kind on your stereo headphones—is also common. In commercial studios, a smaller version of the quarter inch stereo plug, called the Tiny Telephone connector, is also common.

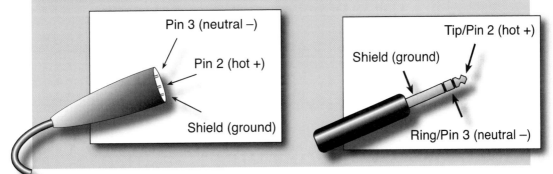

Pin 3 (neutral −)

Pin 2 (hot +)

Shield (ground)

Tip/Pin 2 (hot +)

Shield (ground)

Ring/Pin 3 (neutral −)

Balanced Wiring

Almost all low-impedance mics, as well as some outboard equipment and mixers, use balanced cables. Whereas the length limit of the unbalanced cables is about 25 feet—depending on the position of the moon and the stars—balanced low-impedance cables can be as long as you need (up to 1000 feet or so) without the addition of noise or electrostatic interference and without significant degradation of the audio signal. Pretty cool, huh?!

Previously, we talked about phase interaction. We found that if two waveforms are 180 degrees out of phase, they'll electronically cancel each other. It's also true that if two waveforms are exactly in phase, they'll sum, doubling in amplitude. These two theories play key roles in the design of the balanced system.

A cable for a balanced lo Z mic uses three conductors, unlike the unbalanced system that just uses the hot lead and the braided shield. Of these three conductors, two are used as hot leads and the other is connected to ground. Two-conductor shielded cables are also very common; the two conductors are the hot leads and the shield is connected to ground.

This is the good part, and I'll explain it to you in the simplest illustrative form that I've found. Both hot leads carry the exact same signal. The only difference is that one lead is carrying a signal from the mic that's 180 degrees out of phase with the other lead. This is very significant; knowing this fact is crucial to the understanding of balanced wiring.

If, at any time, you were to cut the cable and combine those two hot leads, you'd hear absolutely no musical signal from the source, since the two hot leads are out of phase; the two sound waves would totally cancel each other. What you would hear would be any noise or electrostatic interference that had been absorbed up to that point. In fact, that noise would be doubled in amplitude from its normal level since both hot leads contain the same interference—completely in phase. The hot leads are twisted evenly throughout the length of the cable intentionally so that they're both subjected to the exact same interference

Any three-point connector can be used on balanced cables. As long as there's a place for the two hot leads and a ground to connect, the system will work. XLR connectors are the most common connector, but a plug like a 1/4" phone stereo headphone plug with a tip-ring-sleeve configuration is also common. In larger commercial studios, a smaller

Balanced Wiring Theory

If the cable were cut anywhere between the connectors, and the hot leads were combined, we'd hear no musical signal; we would hear all noise. This is because the hot leads are 180 degrees out of phase coming from the microphone.

At the mixer, the other hot lead (pin 3), is phase inverted again in order to put the musical signal back in phase with the other hot lead. At the same time this puts the noise 180 degrees out of phase with the noise in the other hot lead; therefore, cancelling any noise picked up throughout the length of the cable.

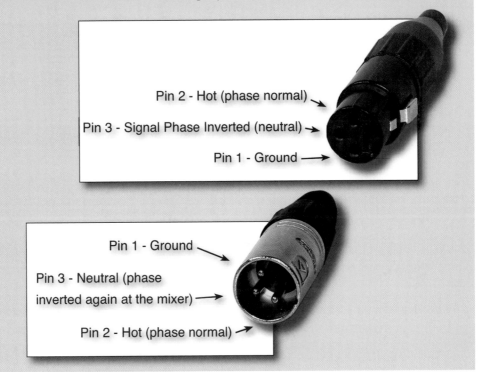

Pin 2 - Hot (phase normal)

Pin 3 - Signal Phase Inverted (neutral)

Pin 1 - Ground

Pin 1 - Ground

Pin 3 - Neutral (phase inverted again at the mixer)

Pin 2 - Hot (phase normal)

version of the stereo phone plug is common: the Tiny Telephone [TT] connector.

Now let's look at the concept of balanced wiring that lets us use cables of up to 1000 feet in length with no significant signal loss and no interference.

I already mentioned that at the microphone end of the cable the two hot leads are carrying the signal 180 degrees out of phase so that if the two hot leads were combined anywhere along the cable length we wouldn't hear any of the desired musical signal. We would, however, hear lots of noise and electrostatic interference.

The completion of the system happens when, at the mixer end of the cable, the phase of one of the hot leads is inverted so that the hot leads are back in phase. Now when they're combined, the signal can be heard, plus there's a doubling in amplitude; this is good.

So what's the benefit of inverting the phase again at the mixer end of the cable, aside from the fact that the hot leads are back in phase?

Since the noise and interference were absorbed throughout the entire length of the cable—no matter how long the cable—and since the noise is absorbed equally and is in phase on both hot leads, a most interesting thing happens when the phase of one of the hot leads is inverted at the mixer end of the cable. Any noise or interference that was picked up by the cable is totally canceled because one of the hot leads contains noise that's made to be 180 degrees out of phase with the noise in the other hot lead. I love that part!

In summary, the result of balanced wiring is total cancellation of noise and interference, plus a doubling in amplitude compared to the signal in an unbalanced system.

Studio Reference Monitors

Studio monitors are reference speakers, designed for specific applications. They provide an accurate audio image at a fairly specific distance and at a normal reference volume. They are different than home entertainment stereo speakers. If you use a typical home stereo speaker as a reference monitor you'll almost always get a sound that's unreliable. Stereo speakers are designed to sound good in a room;

reference monitors are design to provide an accurate image in a normal mix environment.

Selecting speakers is the key to producing good sounds that reliably transfer from your system to a friend's system or your car stereo. One of the most annoying and frustrating audio recording problems is a mix that sounds great on your system but sounds terrible everywhere else.

Part of the solution to this is experience. If you listen, analytically, to enough award-winning music on your system, you'll probably learn to match the basic sound. An even bigger part of the solution to this problem lies in the use of accurate and dependable near-field reference monitors. Industry standards are continually changing and the market for near-field reference monitors has become very competitive. There are great new products available from all major speaker manufacturers, and most are very reasonably priced (typically between $300 and $1000 per pair).

Non-Powered Monitors

A non-powered reference monitor requires an external power amplifier. The speaker enclosure is design to work together with the speakers to provide an accurate sound from a specified distance. Inexpensive models typically contain a passive crossover, which receives the powered signal from an external amplifier. The crossover then divides the full-range signal into two or three frequency ranges, which are then sent to the appropriate speakers. This is the least efficient system.

Some non-powered speakers provide individual access to the high-, mid-, and low-frequency speakers. With this system, you're provided the option of utilizing an external electronic crossover to divide the full-range signal, at line level. Once the frequency ranges are established, they're connected to an external amplifier, which is then connected to the appropriate speaker component. This is a very efficient system.

There is one primary advantage to using non-powered monitors: you can customize your monitoring system. You get to select the monitor you love, combine it with the amplifier(s) you love, and use the cable and connectors you love. This is a wonderful scenario, especially if you like to spend a lot of the money you love.

There are a few disadvantage to using non-powered monitors:

Cost: Especially if your system utilizes an electronic crossover with multiple power amplifiers, the combined cost is substantial.

Efficiency: At home, where budget is a consideration, most people use one stereo power amplifier to send the left and right powered signal to the passive crossover, which is built in to the speaker. This is the least efficient system, especially if you work for hours at a time on your music. The powered signal tends to heat up the crossover components, which, in the course of time, changes their operational characteristic. In other words, they sound different at the end of the session than they do at the beginning.

Ambient noise: Many high-quality power amplifiers require a cooling fan. Most commercial studios keep noisemakers, like amplifiers, CPUs, and tape machines, in a separate room so the actual monitor environment is as free as possible from extraneous ambient noise.

Professional Amplifiers

Connecting the mixer to your power amp is an important step. Use high-quality cables to connect the outputs of the mixer to the inputs of the power amp. Always use balanced connections whenever possible. You'll get a better and more accurate signal that's free from radio interference and other noise. Many wires are specially designed for minimal signal loss. This means a better signal-to-noise ratio. Quality wires and connectors also last longer and create fewer problems.

Crossovers and Amplifiers

Speaker Components*: Studio reference monitors split the audible spectrum into two, three, or even four frequency bands and send each band to a separate component, often called a driver or simply a speaker. Each driver is optimized to reproduce its given band. Large speakers, called woofers, handle low frequencies; mid-sized cone speakers or horns typically handle the mid frequencies; high-frequency horns, dome-tweeters, or even piezo speakers handle the highs.*

Passive Crossove*r: Many reference monitors contain a built-in circuit which receives the full-range, powered signal from an amplifier. This circuit, called a passive crossover, splits the full-range signal into multiple bands which feed the speaker components. The passive cross-over is not a powered circuit. It simply filters the full-range signal into bands.*

Electronic Crossover*: An electronic crossover, like the passive crossover, splits the full-range signal into bands; however, it uses active, powered electronic circuitry to reconstruct or even enhance the bands at line level, not amplified speaker level. The electronic crossover is typically adjustable in each band to adjust to optimize the signal sent to each loudspeaker component.*

Multiamplification*: Typically, the full bandwidth is divided into two or three bands with each band feeding a separate amplifier, which, in turn, powers the appropriate driver. Biamplification (two bands) and triamplification (three bands) are the most common multiamplification configurations.*

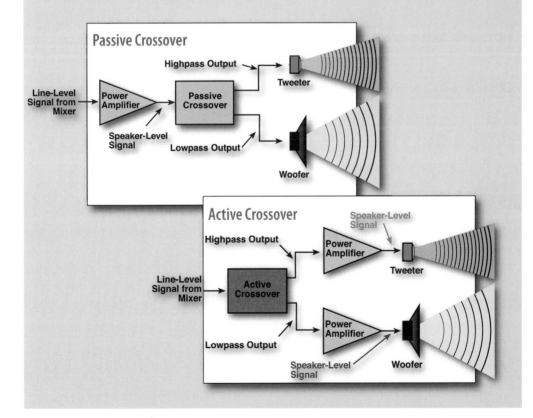

Using a quality power amp is very important. Distortion is a primary cause of ear fatigue, and an amplifier that produces less distortion over longer periods of time causes less fatigue and damage to your ears.

If you have a professional power amp with a rating of at least 100 watts RMS, and if you use a good quality reference monitor designed for studio use, you'll be able to work on your music longer with less ear fatigue. When I use the term professional in regard to amplifiers, I mean an industrial strength unit, designed for constant use in a pro setting. Compared to a consumer home amplifier, amps designed for pro use generally have better specifications, therefore helping to reduce ear fatigue. They use high-quality components, therefore lasting longer and working harder for longer periods of time. Reputable manufacturers offer the best service and support. Fast, quality service is invaluable when you're making money with your equipment.

Using a small system designed for home entertainment is unacceptable for monitoring during any recording project. It's always a great idea to check your mix on a small home stereo system, to verify that it sounds good in that environment; however, if you want your music to sound good in a variety of listening environments, you need a good set of monitors and a trustworthy amplifier.

Self-Powered Monitors

A self-powered monitor has the amplifier built right into the speaker cabinet. Typically, the amplifier mounts to the back of the actual speaker enclosure. This is very convenient and efficient.

A number of years ago, self-powered monitors were very expensive and really not justifiable by most home recording enthusiasts. However, they were very reliable, efficient, and accurate. This is an excellent case, where manufacturing, market demand, and technology came together to make self-powered monitors available and affordable. Now, virtually all manufacturers make self-powered studio monitors designed perfectly for any near-field application.

There are several advantages offered by the self-powered monitor over non-powered models:

+   They are very cost-efficient. Since all the components are designed to work together, the production process is streamlined, keeping manufacturing costs down and quality up.

+   They are very easy to connect. Simple supply AC power and connect a cable from the mixer output to the speaker input.

+   They are very efficient. The amplifier is designed to match the speakers and the box.

+   Since the amplifiers are efficient and small, they don't require cooling fans—they don't add to the ambient noise level. If you aren't cranking out the hits, they're silent.

+   For two- and three-way monitors, the frequency ranges are typically divided (crossed over) prior to the amplifier stage. This is more important than it might seem. Once the crossover divides the full-range signal into two or three ranges, those signals are sent to separate amplifiers, which in turn power the individual components. Whereas, the passive crossover, in a non-powered monitor, changes characteristic when used continuously, the powered system provides a monitor that's consistent and accurate for long periods at a time.

There are few disadvantages to the self-powered monitor, especially for home use. They're affordable, efficient, and they sound good. However, if you have an unlimited budget and lots of time to spare, there are a lot of wonderful components that you can combine for a truly amazing listening experience.

Power Ratings

Power ratings are expressed in watts. It is very important to know something about two types of watts in order to make any assessment about amplifiers.

PMPO stands for Peak Maximum Power Output, usually referred to as simply *peak power*. Peak power lasts only for short durations during momentary blasts of power. Manufacturers sometimes refer to the peak power rating to impress the prospective customer. Peak power ratings are fairly meaningless in our assessment of power amplifiers.

RMS (root mean square) power represents the average sustained power output. RMS is the important power specification for our consideration. The peak power rating is typically at least twice the RMS rating.

Power ratings are a logarithmic function. Since they follow a logarithmic scale, mental comparisons between power ratings are a little confusing at first. In order to make a 3 dB boost, twice the power is required. Since 1 dB is essentially the smallest audible difference in volume, 3 dB just doesn't add up to much, especially considering the power requirements to achieve it. To increase the level by 6 dB, a fourfold power increase is necessary.

Near-Field Reference Monitors

A near-field reference monitor should be used with your head at one point of an equilateral triangle (approximately three feet, or one meter, on each side) and the speakers at the other two points. The speakers should be facing directly at your ears and are ideally about 10 degrees above the horizontal plane that's even with your ears. With this kind of a system, the room that you're monitoring in has a minimal effect on how you hear the mix. These monitors should sound pretty much the same in your studio at home as they do in any studio in the world.

If the room is minimally affecting what you hear, then the mix that you create will be more accurate and will sound good on more systems. Changing to a near field reference monitor gives you immediate gratification through more reliable mixes, plus it lets you start gaining experience based on a predictable and accurate listening environment.

Not just any small speaker works as a near-field reference monitor. In fact, speakers that aren't designed specifically for this application produce poor results and unreliable mixes when positioned as near-field reference monitors.

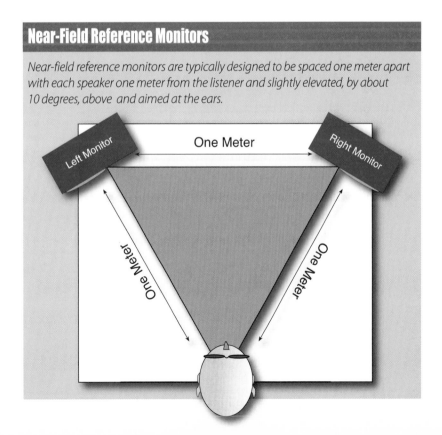

Near-Field Reference Monitors

Near-field reference monitors are typically designed to be spaced one meter apart with each speaker one meter from the listener and slightly elevated, by about 10 degrees, above and aimed at the ears.

Far-Field Monitors

Far-field monitors are designed to be farther away from the engineer, and their sound is greatly affected by the acoustics of the room they're in. Larger rooms have more air to move, so they require larger monitors to move that air. These monitors can be very expensive.

In order to get great results from far-field monitors, they must be used in a studio that has been acoustically designed for a smooth and even balance of frequencies within the room. Since this can involve actual construction, and often plenty of expense, and since near-field reference monitors can produce excellent results, the obvious choice for most home setups is a pair of near-field reference monitors.

Connectors

We encounter several types of connectors when hooking audio equipment together. In this section, we cover RCA connectors, 1/4-inch

RCA Phono Connectors

RCA phono connectors are most typically used in home stereo configurations. They're small, inexpensive, and are not usually used in a professional application. With one contact for the hot lead and one for the shield, this connector is used in an unbalanced application.

connectors, XLR connectors, adapters, plugging in, powering up/down, grounding and hums.

RCA Connectors

RCA phono connectors are the type found on most home stereo equipment and are physically smaller in size than the plug that goes into a guitar or keyboard. RCA phono connectors are among the least expensive connectors and were very common in home-recording equipment manufactured in the mid '80s to the mid '90s. By today's standard, though they are seldom used for serious audio connection. They are only applicable for unbalanced applications and virtually always used for high impedance connections.

1/4" Phone Plug Tip-Sleeve (Mono/Unbalanced)

The 1/4" phone plug is most commonly used in an instrument cable. A regular guitar or keyboard is connected to an amplifier or mixer line input with a cable utilizing a 1/4" phone connector at each end. This connector carries an unbalanced, mono signal. Additionally, phone plugs are often used for speaker cables, using speaker wire rather than line-level instrument cable.

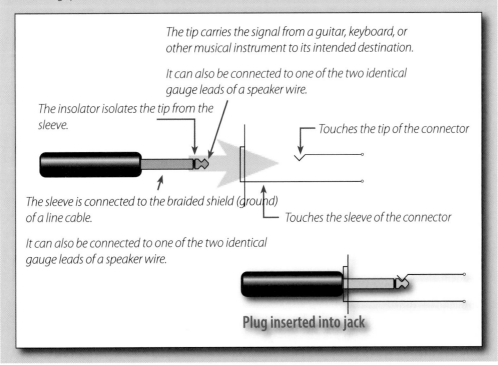

The tip carries the signal from a guitar, keyboard, or other musical instrument to its intended destination.

It can also be connected to one of the two identical gauge leads of a speaker wire.

The insolator isolates the tip from the sleeve.

Touches the tip of the connector

The sleeve is connected to the braided shield (ground) of a line cable.

Touches the sleeve of the connector

It can also be connected to one of the two identical gauge leads of a speaker wire.

Plug inserted into jack

Quarter-Inch Phone Connectors

Quarter-inch phone connectors are the type found on regular cables for guitars or keyboards. These connectors are commonly used on musical instruments and in home and professional recording studios.

Notice that a guitar cable has one tip and one sleeve on the connector. In a guitar cable, the wire connected to the tip carries the actual musical signal. The wire carrying the signal is called the hot wire or hot lead. The sleeve is connected to the braided shield that's around the hot

1/4" Phone Plug Tip-Ring-Sleeve (Stereo/Balanced)

The 1/4" tip-ring-sleeve phone plug is most commonly seen on stereo headphones. In this application, the tip and ring connections carry the left and right channels of a stereo headphone send. This connector, like the XLR, is also commonly used to carry balanced signals, where the tip and sleeve carry the audio signal like pins 2 and 3 of the XLR connector.

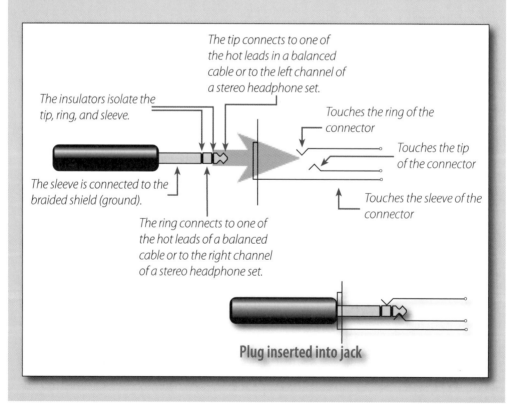

The tip connects to one of the hot leads in a balanced cable or to the left channel of a stereo headphone set.

The insulators isolate the tip, ring, and sleeve.

Touches the ring of the connector

Touches the tip of the connector

The sleeve is connected to the braided shield (ground).

Touches the sleeve of the connector

The ring connects to one of the hot leads of a balanced cable or to the right channel of a stereo headphone set.

Plug inserted into jack

wire. The purpose of the shield is to diffuse outside interference, like electrostatic interference and extraneous radio signals.

The other type of 1/4" phone connector is the type found on stereo headphones. This plug has one tip, one small ring (next to the tip), and a sleeve. These connectors are referred to as 1/4" TRS (Tip-Ring-Sleeve). In headphones, the tip and ring are for the left and right musical signal, and the sleeve is connected to the braided shield that surrounds the two hot wires. The 1/4" TRS connector is also commonly used for balanced line-level connections.

This connector can be used for other devices that require a three-point connection.

XLR Connectors

XLR connectors are the type found on most microphones and the mic inputs of most mixers. Two of the three pins on this connector carry the signal, and the third is connected to the shield. The cable that uses XLR connectors typically carries a balanced signal, utilizing two hot leads and a shield.

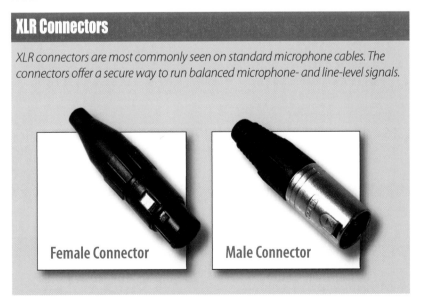

XLR Connectors

XLR connectors are most commonly seen on standard microphone cables. The connectors offer a secure way to run balanced microphone- and line-level signals.

Female Connector   **Male Connector**

It's not uncommon to find cables with an XLR on one end and a 1/4-inch phone plug on the other, or cables that have been intentionally wired in a nonstandard way. These are usually for specific applications and can be useful in certain situations. Check wiring details in your equipment manuals to see if these will work for you.

There are other types of connectors, but RCA phono, 1/4-inch phone, and XLR are the most common. It's okay to use adapters to go from one type of connector to another, but always be sure to use connectors and adapters with the same number of points. For example, if a plug has a tip, ring, and sleeve, it must be plugged into a jack that accepts all three points in order to maintain a consistent function. In some cases, a balanced source (XLR or TRS) delivers an unbalanced signal to an input. This is accomplished by simply connecting one hot lead at the input.

Dual Banana Connectors

Dual banana connectors are typically used on speaker cables, often connecting at the amplifier output and at the speaker enclosure input. This connector is quick and easy to use and to assemble. There is a tab on the negative pole to verify polarity.

Dual Banana Connector

The Dual Banana Connector

Dual banana connectors are a very common speaker wire connector, either at the amplifier output of the speaker box input. They are quickly connected and simple to use. One side has a tab to help keep track of consistent phasing between speaker boxes, or when phase reversal is necessary, they can be flipped upside down. They're also available in various colors so color coordination of frequency splits or amplifier runs are easy. This connector is not used for line-level connections.

Speakon Connectors

Speakon connectors are used for speaker wire termination. Prior to common adoption of the Speakon connector, the dual banana connector was most common. European regulatory requirements outlawed the use of the dual banana connector, forcing the user to terminate with spade lugs or bare wire ends. This prompted the use of the Speakon connection, which has become very common speaker box termination. This connector typically utilizes a four point connection letting the user pass both high and low frequencies of a biamplification scheme

Speakon Connectors

These quick and convenient connectors are typically used for speaker enclosure connections. They offer a multiple pin (4 or 8 points) configuration which provides a simple way to connect to cabinets with bi- and triamplified requirements. Each band is run through the same multi-pair cable.

Speakon Connector

Adapters

The center post on the RCA phono plug corresponds to the tip on the RCA-to-1/4" phone plug adapter.

The tip and the ring on the 1/4" tip-ring-sleeve phone plug correspond to pins 2 and 3 on the 1/4" phone plug-to-XLR adapter. The sleeve corresponds to pin 1. The pin numbers of the XLR connector are imprinted on the connector end itself. They're located next to the base of the pins on the male XLR connector and next to the holes on the female XLR connector.

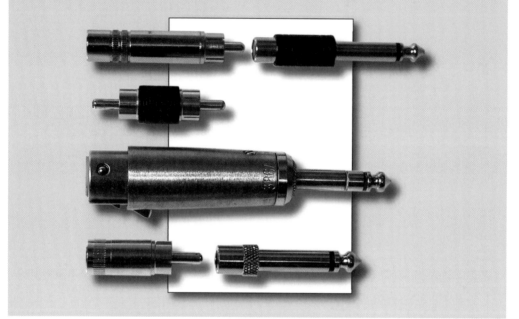

down the same speaker cable, or simply utilize two of the points for a standard speaker connection. The Speakon connector can also be plugged in upside down for the occasion where reversed polarity is desired or necessary.

These connectors are also available in an 8-point version, providing numerous options for multiple-amplification sends. Speakon connector offer a secure, twist-lock connection; and they're fast, easy, and cost-effective. They are not used for line-level sends.

Plugging In

The output of your mixer might have multiple outputs for connection to different amplifier inputs. The stereo line output is the correct output from the mixer to be plugged into the power amplifier. This might also be labeled Main Output, Mains, Mix Out, Control Room Monitor Output, Out to Amp, or Stereo Out. If your mixer has XLR outputs available and if your power amp has XLR inputs, patch these points together as your first choice. This output typically provides the most clean and noise-free signal. Many mixers and amplifiers use 1/4" connectors that are capable of producing or receiving either unbalanced or balanced signals. Use balanced connections wherever possible. If you need to use unbalanced connections, remember to use the shortest cables possible to avoid radio interference and extraneous noises.

Electrical Power

When plugging into the power outlet, use power strips that have protection against power surges and spikes. These can be picked up for a reasonable price at most electrical supply stores.

Spikes and surges are fluctuations in your electrical current that rise well above the 120-volt current that runs most of your equipment. Surges generally last longer than spikes, but both usually occur so quickly that you don't even notice them. Since power surges and spikes can seriously damage delicate electronic circuits, protection is necessary for any microprocessor-controlled equipment (computers, synthesizers, mixers, processors, sequencers, printers, etc.).

Powering Up

+ Turn on the mixer and outboard gear (like delays, reverberation devices and compressors) before the power amps.

+ Always turn power amps on last to protect speakers from pops and blasts as the rest of the electronic gear comes on.

Powering Down

+ Turn power amps off first to protect speakers, then turn the mixer and outboard gear off.

Ground Hum

Aside from causing physical pain, grounding problems can induce an irritating hum into your audio signal. If you have ever had this kind of noise show up mysteriously and at the worst times in your recordings, you know what true frustration is.

Audio Example 2-10

60-Cycle Hum

Sixty-cycle hum is the result of a grounding problem where the 60-cycle electrical current from the wall outlet is inducing a 60-cycle-per-second tone into your musical signal.

The Sine Wave

There are 360° in the complete cycle of a sine wave. This is the simplest wave form, having a smooth crest and trough plus complete symmetry between positive and negative air pressure.

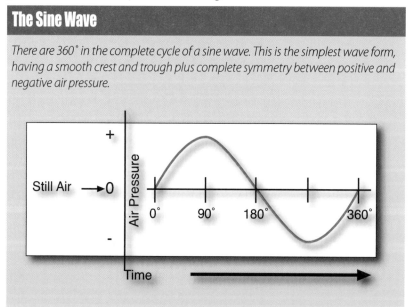

To make matters worse, this 60-cycle tone isn't just a pure and simple 60 Hertz sine wave. A sine wave is the simplest wave form and, in fact, is the only wave form that has a completely smooth crest and trough as it completes its cycle. We could easily eliminate a 60-cycle sine wave with a filter. Sixty-cycle hum has a distinct and distracting wave form, which also includes various harmonics that extend into the upper frequencies.

It's very important to have your setup properly grounded in order to eliminate 60-cycle hum and for your own physical safety while operating your equipment. For some practical solutions to some grounding problems.

Grounding

Grounding is a very important consideration in any recording setup! The purpose of grounding is safety. If there's an electrical short, or a problem in a circuit, the electricity may search out a path other than the one intended. Electricity is always attracted to something connected to the ground we walk on (the earth). The reason for the third pin, called the ground pin, on your AC power cable is to give an electrical problem like this somewhere to go—it provides a low-resistance path for fault current so that circuit protection mechanisms operate quickly.

The ground pin in your electrical wiring is ideally connected, through the third pin on your power cord, to a grounding rod, which is a metal rod that's stuck at least six feet into the earth. Another possible source of ground is a metal pipe like the water supply pipe to your hot water heater. This can be an excellent ground, but be sure the metal pipe at the heater is not connected to plastic pipe before it gets to ground.

If you happen to touch equipment that isn't properly grounded, and if you are standing on the ground, you become just the path to the ground that the electricity is looking for. This could, at the very least, be painful or, at worst, even fatal. Properly grounding a piece of equipment gives potentially damaging electrical problems a path, other than you, to ground. Grounding, while providing essential safety, offers potential signal noise through the formation of ground loops.

Ground Loops

Any time we connect multiple electrical components together (outboard equipment, mixers, amplifiers, etc.) we run the risk of experiencing a ground loop. In the audio world, ground loops cause hums and buzzes; in the video world they cause interference bars in the picture. Functionally, ground loops often cause erratic operation or even damage to audio and video equipment.

In its simplest form, ground loops are caused when your electrical grounds, within your system, aren't at the same electrical potential, specifically zero volts AC and DC. I'll spare you from the long version on this topic. When the ground wire from each outlet to the circuit panel and even the ground lead from your cable TV supplier interconnect there is an excellent likelihood that some ground wires have developed differing electrical potentials. When connected together through your audio and video system connections, a signal degrading, hum-producing, buzz-causing accumulation of 60-cycle hum is given the opportunity to thrive.

Solutions to Grounding Problems

Let's look at some practical solutions to the persistent hums and buzzes that vex so many recording setups. Once your studio is on the right path electrically, your frustration level should drop significantly.

Connect All Equipment to the Same Outlet

This is the simplest and safest solution to this common problem. Since the ground loop is caused by the differences in electrical potential (accumulated voltage) between outlets in your building, plugging into one outlet with all of your equipment drastically reduces the likelihood of grounding problems. This is a problem whenever you're using high-powered amplifiers for your monitor system because you might have too much drain on the circuit. However, most project studios, utilizing self-powered reference monitors shouldn't have a problem connecting everything to one outlet.

Always use high-quality AC distribution. Plastic electrical power strips are known to present a fire threat so use metal power boxes capable of handling your equipment. It's a good idea to hire an electrician to design an appropriate electrical distribution system.

Hire a Pro

The best approach to a persistent grounding problem is to hire a qualified electrician to rewire your studio so that all available electrical outlets have the ground terminals running to the exact same perfect ground.

The ideal situation is to have a completely separate electrical feed run into your studio by the power company. These circuits should be filtered and relayed. When designed properly, if there is a loss of power, circuits will come back on in an order determined by the relay network. It's also a great idea to have any computer-based gear on a power backup system. These backup systems have battery power that will continue the flow of current to your equipment if there's a power loss or failure. You only need to be saved once by one of these systems to be a firm believer in their use.

This solution is obviously impractical for most home users. You might spend as much money to get a truly professional electrical system as many home recordists spend on their recording equipment altogether. Please keep in mind, though, that you might benefit greatly by a simple consultation with an experienced electrical technician.

Lifting the Ground

Lifting the ground is accomplished when the third prong on an AC power cable does not plug into the power outlet.

The ground can be lifted on any piece of gear that has a three-prong wall plug by plugging that wall plug into a small adapter that accepts all three prongs from the power chord at the in end but only has two prongs coming out of the out end. If the power cord has only two prongs, the ground has already been lifted.

AC Plug into Ground Lifter

An inconsistency in ground and in-house wiring can produce a low hum in your audio signal. When this happens, you can use a ground lifter on the piece of equipment causing the hum. The ground lifter is the adapter that accepts all three prongs from a standard AC cable but turns the ground pin into a tab. This tab can be screwed to the wall plate mounting screw if the ground needs to be completed at the outlet, or if you need the ground disconnected at that point, simply bend the ground tab back and leave it disconnected.

Possible danger! Consult a qualified electrician about your unique setup.

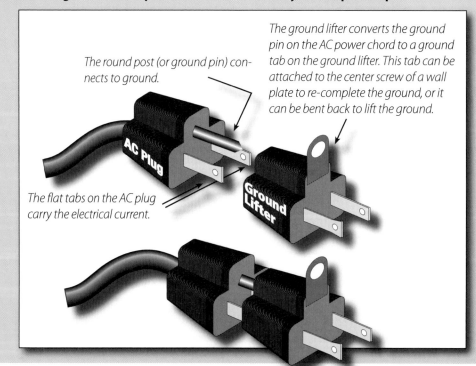

The round post (or ground pin) connects to ground.

The ground lifter converts the ground pin on the AC power chord to a ground tab on the ground lifter. This tab can be attached to the center screw of a wall plate to re-complete the ground, or it can be bent back to lift the ground.

The flat tabs on the AC plug carry the electrical current.

Lifting the ground doesn't necessarily mean that nothing is grounded; it simply means that a particular piece of equipment isn't grounded twice to conflicting grounds. Many home studios have the ground lifted on all pieces of gear except one. In such a case, all gear that's part of the network grounds to that one piece, even though their individual power cord grounds aren't connected.

If all grounds are lifted, it's advisable to connect all of the individual chassis grounds together with zip cord, lamp wire, or #10 insulated wire. Most pieces of equipment have ground terminals on their back panels. If there is no ground terminal, connect the ground wire to any screw that goes into the metal chassis. It's easiest if you connect all of these wires to one terminal strip, mounted close to your gear, then connect the terminal strip to a true ground. A true ground can be difficult to find, but try the hot water supply pipe to your hot water tank, the center screw on one of your wall AC outlet face plates, or have an electrician install and verify a true ground source.

Disconnect Shield at the Destination

Another way to eliminate hum is to disconnect the shield at one end of your line cable (patch cable, instrument cable, guitar cord, etc.), usually at the end closest to your mixer. This can break the ground loop and solve the problem. To disconnect the shield on a cable, you must open the connector and either cut or unsolder the braided shield from the lug or pin it's connected to. It can be convenient to keep a couple of cables like this around. Mark them clearly and indicate the end with the disconnected shield.

Circuit Tester

Most electrical stores should stock a circuit tester, designed to verify that the AC circuit from the wall has been wired correctly. If you see any deviation from standard wiring when the tester is plugged into the wall outlet, don't use the circuit.

Danger, Danger

Anyone who has ever played in a real live garage band knows that there's always danger when electrical equipment, musicians, and cement floors coexist. The cement floor is connected directly to the ground, and you can become a very attractive option for electricity in search of ground if you're standing on the cement. Remember, the human body can conduct the flow of 20 to 30 amps of 110-volt alternating current (AC). Since this can be, at the very least, very painful or, at worst, even lethal, *be cautious*.

Proper grounding can be the single most important factor in keeping your system quiet and buzz free. A poorly designed system can have many hums and other unwanted sounds and noises. Paying attention to detail here and hiring some professional help will make your home studio far more functional and tons more fun.

Keep in mind that you've just seen some practical solutions to common problems, but a professional electrician should handle electrical wiring and system design. Studio grounding is a specialized application, so look for an electrician with expertise in this field. Hiring the right electrician with the right bag of tricks for the studio is a very worthwhile investment.

The Mixer

You must understand everything about your mixer! Most modern mixers offer ample headroom and abundant features. The better your understanding of the primary mixer functions, the better your chances of experiencing creative freedom.

Input Levels

Audio Example 3-1 is mixed three different ways—same music and board but different mixes. Notice the dramatic differences in the effect and feeling of these mixes. Even though they all contain the same instrumentation and orchestration, the mixer combined the available textures differently in each example.

Audio Example 3-1

Comparison of Three Different Versions of the Same Mix

The mixer is where your songs are molded and shaped into commercially and artistically palatable commodities. If this is all news to you, there's a long and winding road ahead. We'll take things a step at a time, but for now you need to know what the controls on the mixer do. No two mixers are set up in exactly the same way, but the concepts involved with most mixers are essentially the same.

In this section, we'll cover those concepts and terms that relate to the signal going to and coming out of the mixing board. These concepts include

*   High and low impedance
*   Direct boxes and why they're needed
*   Phantom power
*   Line levels

A mixer is used to combine, or mix, different sound sources. These sound sources might be

*   On their way to the multitrack
*   On their way to effects from instruments or microphones
*   On their way from the multitrack to the monitor speakers, effects or mixdown machine

We can control a number of variables at a number of points in the pathway from the sound source to the recorder and back. This pathway is called the signal path. Each point holds its own possibility for degrading or enhancing the audio integrity of your music.

Input Stage

Let's begin at the input stage, where the mics and instruments plug into the mixer. Mic inputs come in two types: high impedance and low impedance. There's no real difference in sound quality between these two as long as each is used within its limitations.

In practical application, microphone connections are almost always low impedance, especially in the recording studio, whereas, instrument outputs are typically high impedance. In order to plug a guitar or keyboard into a microphone input, you must incorporate a line matching transformer.

The main concern when considering impedance is that high-impedance outputs go into high-impedance inputs and low-impedance outputs go into low-impedance inputs.

To review what we studied in the previous chapter, impedance is, by definition, the resistance to the flow of current measured in a unit called an ohm. Imagine two pipes: one large and one small. More water can go through the large pipe with less resistance than the same amount of water through the small pipe. I think we would all agree that a city water reservoir would be easier to drain through a six-foot diameter pipe than through a straw. The large pipe represents low impedance (low resistance). The small pipe represents high impedance (high resistance).

We put a numerical tag on impedance. High impedance has high resistance, in the range of 10,000 to 20,000 ohms (a small pipe). Low impedance has low resistance, in the range of 150–1000 ohms (a large pipe).

A high-impedance instrument plugged into a low-impedance input is expecting to see lots of resistance to its signal flow. If the signal doesn't meet that resistance, it'll overdrive and distort the input almost immediately, no matter how low you keep the input level.

A low-impedance mic plugged into a high-impedance input meets too much resistance to its signal flow. Therefore, no matter how high you turn the input level up, there's insufficient level to obtain a proper amount of VU reading. The water from the large pipe can't all squeeze into the small pipe fast enough.

Output Impedance

There is a difference between input and output impedance. In days when everything was centered on the vacuum tube (an inherently high-impedance device), it was most efficient and financially feasible to match input and output impedances. In the early 1900s, Bell Laboratories found that to achieve maximum power transfer in long distance telephone circuits, the impedances of interconnected devices should be matched. Impedance matching reduced the number of vacuum tube amplifiers needed. Since these amplifying circuits produced a lot of heat, were expensive, and bulky there was sufficient motivation to do whatever it took to match impedances.

Output Impedance versus Input Impedance

It's alright to split outputs, typically up five or more times, to send a signal to multiple destinations. It's not okay to simply combine multiple sources to a signal input without a specific summing matrix like the output bus selector on your mixer.

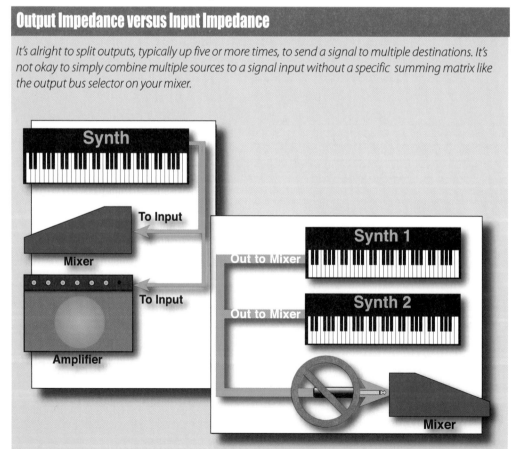

Bell Laboratories invented a small cheap amplifier, called the transistor in 1948. With the advent of the transistor (an inherently low-impedance device), everything changed. The transistor utilizes maximum voltage transfer where the destination device (called the *load*) should have an impedance at least 10 times that of the sending device (the *source*). This concept, known as *bridging,* is the most common circuit configuration used to connect audio devices.

Because of the load-source relationship it is possible to simply split one output several times for connection to multiple inputs. Conversely, summing multiple sending signals (sources) to one destination device (load) is not recommended. It's necessary to utilize a summing circuit to combine multiple sources to a load.

Speaker Impedance

Speakers also exhibit impedance characteristics, which must be matched to the amplifier outputs. Amplifiers are rated according to the load range of the source. Most amplifiers specify minimum operational impedance. The components of a speaker box are wire together an a way that produces the desired load (the impedance at the input enclosure's connector).

Impedance math is pretty simple. Each amplifier is rated at minimum impedance, which is typically 4 or 8 Ω. You simply need to be are of the impedance load you putting on the amplifier to optimize the power output and rating. Never connect speakers in such a way that the impedance load is less than the specified minimum. If the speaker offers too little resistance to the amplifier signal, it's just like trying to push a little water through a big pipe—it can't sustain the push and eventually will overheat and fail. Proper impedance matching provides a balance, which results in the efficient transfer of power.

Calculating Speaker Impedance Loads

There are two ways to wire speakers (also commonly called *drivers*) together: in *parallel* and in *series*.

Multiple speakers wired in parallel present a lower impedance load to the amplifier output. To calculate the resulting impedance, divide each

Parallel and Series Wiring

Two speakers, equal in load, wired in parallel cut the impedance load in half. Two speakers, equal in load, wired in series double the impedance load.

*Where "S" equals speaker impedance, the equations used to calculate the resulting impedance from a parallel connection is Load=S1 * S2÷(S1+S2)*

The equations used to calculate the impedance resulting from a series connection is: Load=S1+S2+S3…

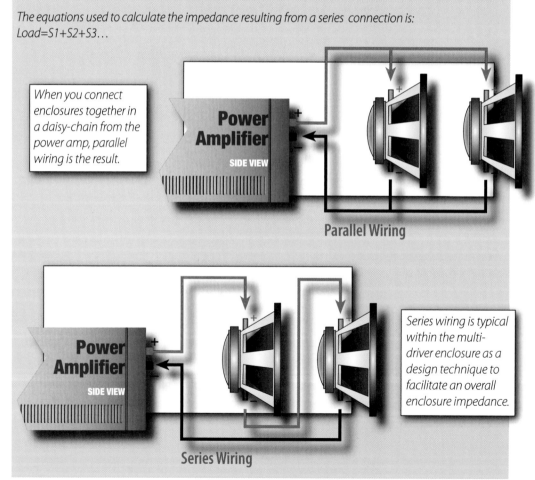

When you connect enclosures together in a daisy-chain from the power amp, parallel wiring is the result.

Parallel Wiring

Series wiring is typical within the multi-driver enclosure as a design technique to facilitate an overall enclosure impedance.

Series Wiring

speaker's impedance by the number of speakers. Two 8-ohm speakers wired together in parallel result in a 4-ohm load. Parallel connections are the most common between multiple speaker cabinets. This is the kind of connection you're making when you use a speaker cable to daisy chain boxes, or when you stack dual banana connectors. In this scenario the positive post on each speaker input is connected together to the positive post on the amplifier output. Also, both negative speaker inputs are connected to the amplifier negative post

Series wiring is more common in internal speaker design using multiple drivers in a single enclosure, or whenever a large array is designed for certain applications. Multiple speakers wired in series present a higher impedance load to the amplifier output. To calculate the resulting impedance of two speakers wired in series the load presented to the amplifier output is double each speaker's individual impedance. Two 4-ohm speakers wired in series presents an 8-ohm load to the amplifier. Series wiring completes a circuit from the positive post amplifier output, through two speakers and back to the negative post on the amplifier. The positive post on the amplifier connects to the positive side of speaker 1; the negative side of speaker 1 connects to the positive side of speaker 2; then, the negative side of speaker 2 connects to the negative post on the amplifier.

Bridging an Amplifier

There are some instances, especially in system design where the audible frequency spectrum is divided into bands for delivery to optimized drivers and/or enclosures, where a stereo amplifier is transformed into a more powerful mono amp, through bridging. Bridging combines the left-right output from the power amplifier into a mono output with increased power.

Be sure that the power amplifier is designed to be bridged. Any amplifier is easily bridged by simple connection modification, but if the amp isn't designed to be bridge it could be damaged.

Bridging the Power Amp Outputs

Be sure your power amplifier is designed to be bridged before you attempt this procedure. If your amp isn't specifically designed for bridging, it will be damaged.

Bridging the stereo outputs results in a mono output with increased power. The power amp below offers two sets of powered outputs: dual banana and Speakon. Using the banana connection in normal stereo mode, the channel one and two red and black terminals connect to the corresponding speaker enclosure terminals. Notice that in mono the single banana connector is flipped horizontally to connect to the positive terminals of channels one and two.

To bridge to mono, simply connect a banana plug to the red posts or select BRIDGE mode and connect to the Speakon MONO BRIDGE output.

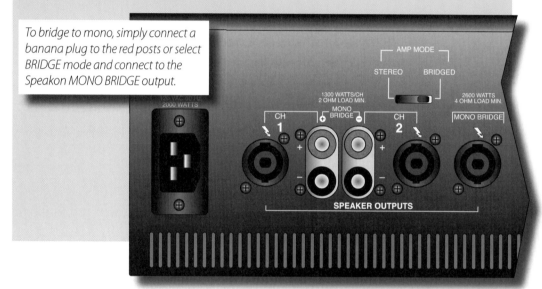

The bridged connection is very simple to accomplish. From the power amplifier connect the positive post from output 1 to the positive post on the enclosure, then connect the positive post from output 2 to the negative post on the enclosure.

Some amplifiers provide a switch to select bridge mode with a diagram showing proper speaker connection. Amplifiers using banana connections typically position the outputs so that bridging is easily accomplished by connecting the plug across the left-right outputs instead of between the positive and negative posts on just one of the outputs.

Direct Box

It's possible, acceptable and standard procedure to use a direct box to match a high-impedance output to a low-impedance input or vice versa. A direct box is also called a line-matching transformer, impedance-matching transformer, impedance transformer or DI (direct injection). Its sole purpose is to change the impedance of the instrument or device plugged into its input.

Impedance transformers work equally well in both directions—low to high or high to low. Using the same transformer, you can plug a high-impedance instrument into the high-impedance input and then patch the low-impedance output into a low-impedance input, or, if necessary, you can plug low-impedance into the low-impedance end and come out of the transformer high-impedance.

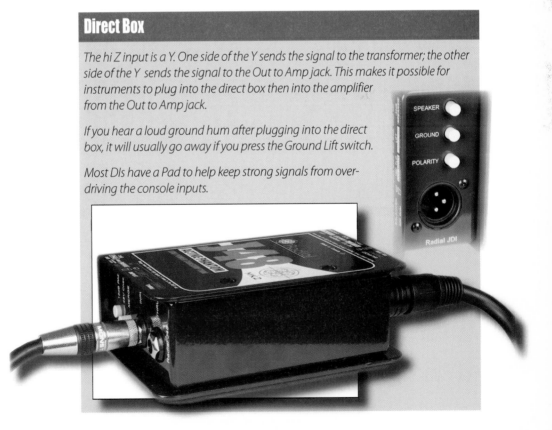

Direct Box

The hi Z input is a Y. One side of the Y sends the signal to the transformer; the other side of the Y sends the signal to the Out to Amp jack. This makes it possible for instruments to plug into the direct box then into the amplifier from the Out to Amp jack.

If you hear a loud ground hum after plugging into the direct box, it will usually go away if you press the Ground Lift switch.

Most DIs have a Pad to help keep strong signals from over-driving the console inputs.

Passive versus Active DIs

There are two main types of direct boxes: passive and active. Passive direct boxes are the least expensive and generally do a fine job of matching one impedance in to another impedance out. Active direct boxes are usually more expensive and contain amplifying circuitry that requires power from a battery or other external power supply. These amplifying circuits are used to enhance bass and treble. An active direct box typically gives your signal more punch and clarity in the high frequencies and low frequencies.

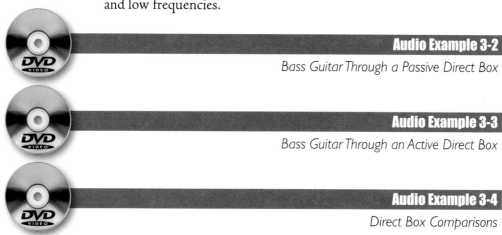

Audio Example 3-2

Bass Guitar Through a Passive Direct Box

Audio Example 3-3

Bass Guitar Through an Active Direct Box

Audio Example 3-4

Direct Box Comparisons

The difference between these two examples can be subtle, but it's often the nuances that make the difference between okay and brilliant! A 10 percent improvement of each track really impacts the final product, especially when recording 8, 16, 24 or more tracks. Optimize every step of your recording process! It makes a noticeable difference.

Direct boxes typically have a ground lift switch. Try flipping this switch if you can hear a noticeable 60-cycle ground hum along with the instrument sound. There is usually one position that eliminates hum.

Phantom Power

Condenser microphones and active direct boxes need power to operate. If they don't receive it, they won't work. This power can come from a battery in the unit or from the phantom power supply located within the mixer.

Phantom power (a very low amperage 48-volt DC current) is available at any mic input that has a phantom power switch. Since amperage is the actual punch behind the voltage and since phantom power has a very low amperage, there's little danger that this power will cause you any physical harm, even though the power travels to the mic or direct box through the same mic cable that the musical signal travels to the mixer.

Phantom power requirements can vary from mic to mic so check your mic specifications to insure that the mic is getting the power it needs. Voltage requirements are typically between 12 and 52 volts. Most mics that require low voltages have a regulatory circuit to reduce higher voltages so that normal 48-volt phantom power can be used without damaging the mic. Microphones that require higher voltages won't usually sound all that great until they get the power they require. These mics often come with their own power supply.

Your mixer might not have phantom power built in. Most microphone manufacturers offer external phantom power supplies for one or more mics. Simply plug the phantom power supply into an AC outlet, and then plug the cable from the mic or direct box into the phantom power supply. Finally, patch from the XLR output of the phantom power supply into the mixer mic input.

Phantom power is preferred over battery power because it is constant and reliable, whereas batteries can wear down, lose power and cause the mic or direct box to operate below its optimum specification (even though it might still be working).

If the mic or direct box doesn't need phantom power, it's good practice to turn the power off on those channels, though it isn't absolutely essential. Many consoles have phantom power on/off switches. Some mixers have phantom power that stays on all of the time. This is okay but if there's an on/off switch, turn it on when you need it and off when you don't.

Mic Level

The effective output of each microphone is typically quantified in relation to line level. Most microphones output a signal that is between 30 and 60 dB below line level. This means that the signal from the microphone must be boost between 30 and 60 dB before the signal strength is at line level and ready to move through the mixer.

Line Level

Line in and line out are common terms typically associated with tape recorder inputs and outputs and mixer inputs and outputs. The signal that comes from a microphone has a strength that's called mic level, and a mixer needs to have that signal amplified to what is called line level. The amplifier that brings the mic level up to line level is called the mic preamp. We'll study mic preamps later in this chapter.

Instrument inputs on mixers are line level. An input that is line level enters the board after the microphone preamp and is, therefore, not affected by its adjustment.

Some mixers have attenuators on the line inputs and the mic inputs to compensate for different instrument and tape recorder output levels. As we optimize each instrument or voice recording, we must optimize the gain structure at each point of the signal path. When all the levels are correct for each mic preamp, line attenuator, fader, EQ, bus fader, etc., we can record the cleanest, most accurate signal. When one link of this chain is weak, the overall sonic integrity crashes and burns.

Mixers that have only one 1/4-inch phone input on each channel typically have a Mic/Line switch. Select the appropriate position for your situation. In mic position, the input goes through the preamp. In line position (possibly called instrument position), the preamp is not included.

Connecting a Professional Microphone to a Computer Sound Card

There is a significant difference between the sound cards used in Apple computers versus the IBM-compatible PC. Most Apple computers have a sound card built in; most IBM-compatible computers require that a sound card is added. There are three key factors that must be discovered and matched between the mic and the computer's sound input:

+ Signal level
+ Electrical impedance
+ Connector type and wiring scheme

Signal Level

Often the sound card input, typically labeled with a small microphone, is better suited to a high-impedance microphone than it is to a professional low-impedance microphone. Whereas, most computer sound inputs require a minimum signal level of at least 1/100th of a volt (10 millivolts) or even more, the average professional microphone typically provides a mere 1/1000th of a volt (1 millivolt).

There are two possible solutions to this level incompatibility:

+ Often, the computer sound card has a level boost built in, which might add sufficient gain to provide adequate level. However, these amplifying circuits often cause an unacceptable noise threshold.
+ Utilizing a microphone preamplifier is typically the best solution. Any small mixer, with microphone inputs, provides adequate preamplification of the mic signal to match the level to any computer sound card input. Plug the microphone into the mixer, then connect the mixer output to the sound card input. By adjusting the mixer output level so that, when the sound card input is set to a normal setting the proper levels are achieved, excellent audio quality is possible.

Impedance

For acceptable results, the output impedance of the microphone must be less than the input impedance of the sound card. If the microphone impedance is the same or higher than the sound card input, some or all of the microphone signal will be lost—this is called *loading*. The higher the microphone signal is, compared to the sound card, the more signal will be lost.

Connectors and Wiring

The most obvious difference between the professional microphone and the computer input is the connector used on each. Simply due to space issues, most computer inputs utilize 1/8th inch mini connections. The standard XLR or 1/4-inch connectors, common to professional mics, are far too large for most computer applications.

Professional microphones with XLR connectors use a balanced wiring scheme, where pins 2 and 3 carry the audio and pin 1 and the shield are connected to ground. Most computers use an unbalanced wiring scheme, which requires only one hot lead. There is no standard wiring for computer sound card inputs, so the actual wiring scheme depends on the manufacturer.

Sound cards typically use either a mono or stereo mini plug or a connection. In the case of a mono mini plug, pin 2 of the XLR should be connected to the tip of the mini plug; XLR pin 3 and the shield should be connected to the sleeve.

In the case of a stereo mini plug, the XLR pin 2 should be connected to the mini plug tip; whereas, the XLR pins 1 and 3 should be connected to the sleeve. It is unnecessary to connect anything to the mini plug ring.

If the microphone requires phantom power, the simplest solution is to use batteries in the mic itself, since most sound cards don't supply

Connecting a Professional Mic to a Mini Plug Computer Input

This wiring scheme works well with microphones that don't require power. Whereas, most mixers provide phantom power to operate condensor microphones, most computer sound cards don't. Use this method to connect the XLR, from the mic, to the computer's mini plug input.

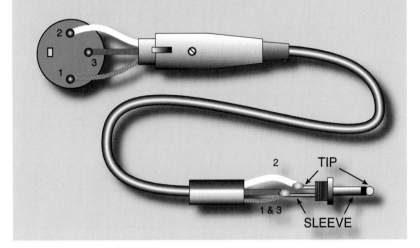

it. It's also possible to use an external phantom power supply or simply use a small mixer to provide phantom power, the proper level, and the correct impedance.

+4 dBm versus –10 dBV

You might have heard the terms plus four or minus 10 (+4 or –10) used when referring to a mixer, tape recorder or signal processor.

This is another consideration for compatibility between pieces of equipment, aside from the low impedance/high impedance dilemma. Different equipment can have different relative line level strength. This level comparison, tagged in dB is specified as either +4 dBm or 12–10 dBV.

When we use the term dB it's useful to keep in mind that it is a term that expresses a ratio between two powers and can be tagged to many different types of power that we encounter in recording.

With our option of +4 dBm, dB is being tagged to milliwatts; and with −10 dBV, dB is being tagged to volts. Without going into the math of it all, let's simply remember that +4 equipment only works well with other +4 equipment, and −10 equipment only works well with other −10 equipment.

Some units let you switch between +4 and −10, so all you do is select the level that matches your system. There are also boxes made that let you go in at one level and out at the other. In many situations, a tool like this is a necessary solution.

Most +4 gear is balanced low-impedance. This is the type that's used in a true blue professional recording studio and uses either an XLR connector or some other type of three-pin connector, like a stereo headphone type of plug (tip-ring-sleeve). Gear can also be of the unbalanced variety and still operate at +4.

We most often think of −10 dBV gear as being unbalanced, although this is not always the case. This type of gear is considered semi-professional. Some home recording equipment operates at −10 dBV. Gear that uses RCA phono plugs or regular mono guitar plugs is typically −10 dBV.

Some pieces of equipment will have a switch somewhere that will let you select whether they operate at +4 or −10. A +4 output is too strong for a −10 input, and a −10 output is too weak for a +4 input.

When used properly and with shorter cable runs, there should not be a noticeable difference in sound quality from a unit operating at −10 as opposed to +4, even though +4 is the professional standard.

+4 dBm balanced equipment works especially well when longer cable runs are necessary, like in a large recording studio, or when radio interference and electrostatic noises are a particular problem.

If you are considering signal processors (reverbs, compressors, gates, etc.), mixers or tape recorders, you must always maintain compatibility between +4 and −10 equipment.

Units are available which allow +4 dBm and −10 dBV gear to work perfectly together. Plug in one end at +4, and the signal comes out the other end at −10, or vice versa.

The Virtual Mixer

A virtual mixer is the mixer built in to your digital audio recording software. Again, like the digital mixer, there aren't really any new functions on these mixers, just on screen representations of the same functions. Sometimes the virtual mixer is more cumbersome to operate, especially if you're not using a very large monitor.

Split versus In-Line Consoles

We begin with the mixing board. Our approach throughout this series is that the mixing board is one of the engineer's musical instruments. Always let the music lead the way through technology. Let your ears and your heart tell you what the musical sounds should be, then use the tools of the trade to get those artistically inspired sounds.

The state of our art has radically changed over the past several years. I actually feel quite privileged to have entered the recording industry at a period now considered historic—in a day when any serious recording was done in a commercial recording studio; where the equipment used was far too expensive for the home recordist to consider; and musical and technical details could only be entrusted to experienced professionals. In those days, a mixer was a solid and stable piece of equipment.

The Virtual Mixer

The virtual mixer is a real mixer that resides in software. In actuality, the modern mixer has become a combination of two components: software interface and hardware control surface. The software interface provides access to all parameters; whereas, the hardware control surface (often optional) provides a means of tactile control. The control surface provides quick and easy access to all audio parameters while feeling like a recording console.

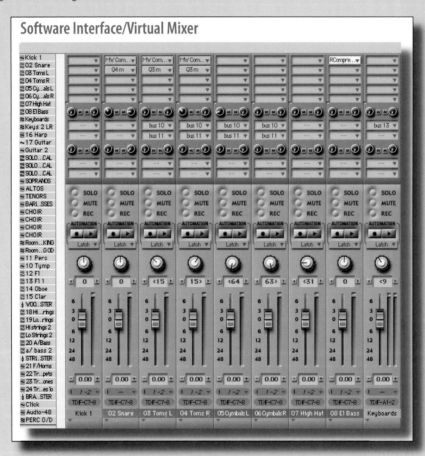

Once you understood its layout and the capabilities, you could rest assured that everyday in the studio you would sit down to the same familiar console. You could learn where to tap which module when a gremlin would raise its ugly, though familiar, head. You could figure out which channel strips sounded best and which ones didn't.

The Split Mixer

I always thought of one studio, at which I was chief engineer for a number of years, as the audio equivalent of the Millennium Falcon in the first Star Wars movie. It was very good in the heat of battle but very temperamental and responsive to only Han Solo. Even though we changed all the capacitors in the console and updated all the integrated circuit chips and really tried to make everything right, I was constantly aware that there were several occasions per day where noises and other dysfunctions became so familiar that without thinking I would end up tapping in one certain corner of the control room monitor module, or re-seating a card in the tape machine, or wiggling a patch cable to remedy an otherwise debilitating glitch.

Today's mixer is often nothing more than a digital grid in which almost anything can happen. You, the user, get to set up the way you work. You control the way audio is routed, the look and feel of the user interface, even the quality and resolution of the audio signal. For the home recordist it's increasingly likely that there is no physical mixer at all. Your mixer might be the virtual mixer within your computer audio recording software. It has become more likely that a physical mixer performs as a control surface for your virtual mixer, offering tactile control over onscreen functions.

The Split Console Design

Let's look at how a typical mixer is laid out. Then we'll study the location and function of each control. Later in this chapter, I'll explain each control in detail so you'll know what each feature is and how it works. The terms mixer, console, board, mixing desk, desk, and audio production console are used interchangeably. In addition, the virtual mixer is the software, onscreen user interface that mirrors while augmenting the functions common to the hardware mixer.

It is very important that you possess a thorough understanding of basic mixer functions, whether you're using a complicated hardware or software mixer. A virtual mixer provides operational features based on, and identical in functionality to, most functions and controls found on a physical mixer. My digital console I use in my project studio has all the same controls I find on the large-format analog consoles I use in the commercial facilities. Software often imitates and emulates the high-quality mixers, manufactured by Solid State Logic, Neve, Trident, etc.

The Split

The split mixer provides input channels that are routed via a switching matrix to the bus outputs. The bus outputs are typically assigned to the left-right main mix, although they can typically be routed to multiple locations, providing maximum flexibility. In tracking mode, the switching matrix supplies signal to the multitrack; in mixdown mode the channels are usually routed directly to the main mix unless the bus outputs are used for sub group control.

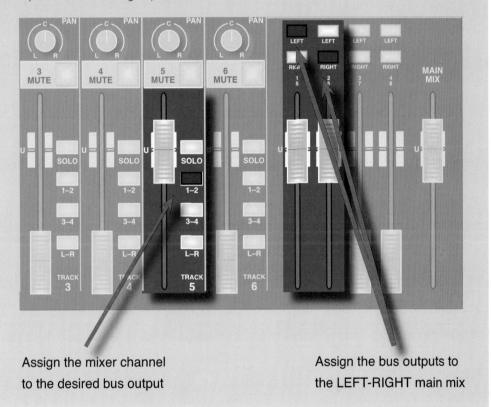

Assign the mixer channel
to the desired bus output

Assign the bus outputs to
the LEFT-RIGHT main mix

Additionally, it has become more likely that established hardware manufacturers are producing their own plug-ins to match both the functionality, and the audio quality of their product.

Mixers have a number of channels, each typically having the same controls. These controls can include an attenuator (also called a pad); a phase switch; a preamp control; auxiliary sends; equalization; a pan control; track assignments; solo, mute and PFL buttons and the

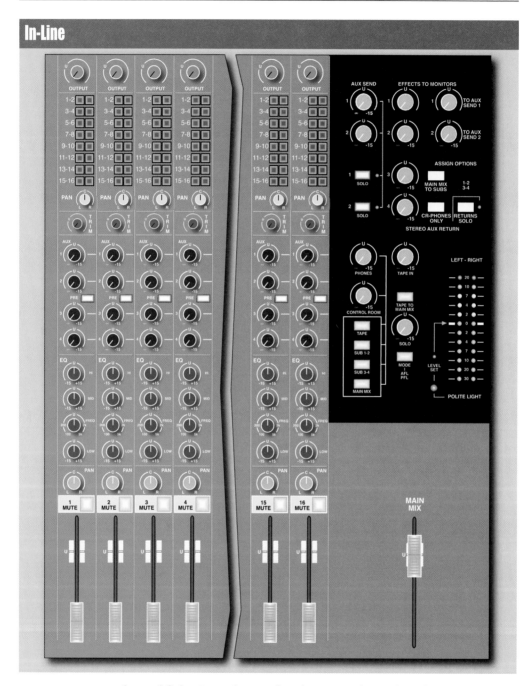

channel fader. In understanding how one channel works, you'll understand how they all work.

To the right of the channels, there is often a monitor section. In the monitor section, there is usually a master volume control for adjusting listening levels, a monitor selector (where we choose what we listen to), master aux send levels, a test tone oscillator, a stereo master fader, a stereo/mono button, a headphone jack and on some mixers, and we also see the output level controls for the track assignment bus.

In-Line Switching Matrix

The in-line console design provides the bus outputs at the top of each channel strip. These are the same controls as the bus faders to the right of the channels in the split console design. In this design the bus assignments are typically paired together—any individual button assigns to the selected bus. When odd and even buses are selected, the pan control moves the channel between odd and even (left and right).

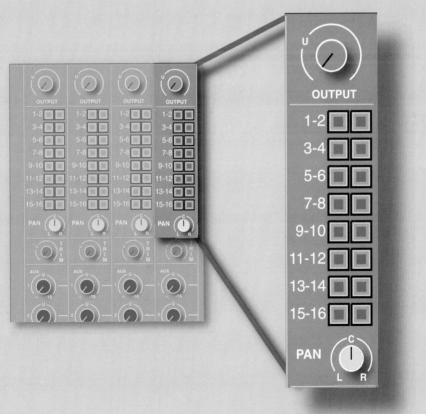

The In-Line Console Design

If your mixer has faders to the right of the channel input faders, and if these faders adjust the level of the final output to the multitrack, then your mixer is called a split mixer or console.

Some mixers have the level controls to the multitrack (typically knobs instead of faders) near the top of each channel. These are called in-line consoles.

Split and in-line mixers each have their own set of advantages, but both can be very effective and flexible while sonically supporting your musical ideas. I've worked a lot on both types and have adjusted quite easily because I understand how each configuration operates. My goal is to explain the basics in simple enough terms that you'll be able to integrate all concepts seamlessly into any recording situation.

Take a look at your mixer to see which kind of controls you have. Identify whether you have a split or in-line mixer.

The Analog versus Digital Mixer

If you possess a thorough understanding of the mixer functions we've just studied, you'll be able to operate efficiently on an analog or digital mixer. With any new mixer, the real test is where all the features are located, not necessarily, what features are available.

The advantage of an analog console is its simplicity. Each channel is the same and the EQ knob is at the same spot on the console each time. Digital mixers are so flexible that it's not always easy to guess where the controls are; they might be hidden somewhere in a tangled web of menus.

The really nice feature of nearly any digital mixer is its ability to store snapshots of the entire mixer layout for retrieval later. It's a simple matter to setup a tracking session and then just save the snapshot of that session. The snapshot contains all EQ, level setting, routing, effects, etc., so resetting for tracking on another day is a simple matter of a button push.

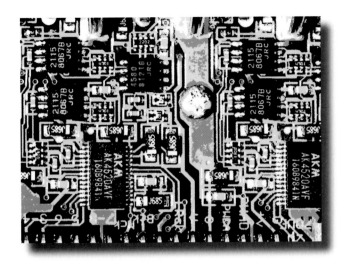

Signal Path

At first glance, mixers can be very intimidating to new users. Don't forget, for the most part each channel has exactly the same controls. So, if we can use and understand one channel, we've already won most of the battle. In this section, we begin to see what each control can do. As you grasp these concepts thoroughly, the mixer becomes a creative tool rather than a formidable adversary.

Signal path is simply the route that a signal takes from point A to point B. For speed and efficiency in any recording situation, it's essential that you're completely familiar with the signal paths involved in your setup. Any good maintenance engineer knows that the only surefire way to find a problem in a system is to follow the signal path deliberately from its point of origin (point A, for example, the microphone) to its destination (point B, the speakers).

There are several possible problem spots between point A and point B. A thorough knowledge and understanding of your signal path lets you deal with any of these problems as quickly as possible.

Many owner's manuals give a schematic diagram of exactly what the signal path is in a mixer. You may not be totally into reading diagrams, but there's a lot to be learned by simply following the arrows and words. The basis of electronics is logic. Most complex electronic tasks can be broken down into small and simple tasks. That's exactly how the recording world is. What seems like an impossible task at first isn't so bad when you realize it consists of several simple tasks performed in the right order.

An example of a typical signal path is as follows: The microphone goes into the microphone input, which goes to the attenuator, which goes into the preamp, which goes into the equalizer, which goes to the track assignment, which goes to the tape recorder, which comes back to the mixer at the monitor section, which goes to the master volume

Signal Path

Many owner's manuals give a schematic diagram of the mixer's signal path. You may not be totally into reading diagrams, but there's a lot to be learned by simply following the arrows and words.

A thorough understanding of your signal path will help you troubleshoot most audio problems. Build a diagram like this for the most common recording situations you encounter, including

- *Recording tracks*
- *Mixing down*
- *Sending from aux buses to effects*
- *Setting up the headphone bus*

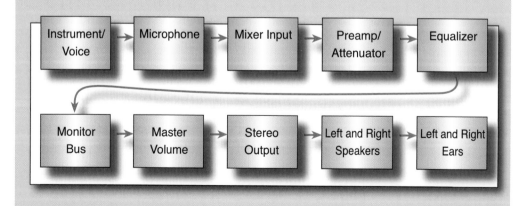

fader, which goes to the main stereo output of the mixer, which goes to the power amp in, which goes to the speakers, which go to your ears, which go to your brain, which makes you laugh or cry. A thorough understanding of your signal path is the answer to most trying circumstances you'll come across.

The Preamp

One of the first things your signal from the mic sees as it enters the mixer is the mic preamp (sometimes called the input preamp or simply the preamp). The preamp is actually a small amplifier circuit, and its controls are generally at the top of each channel. The preamp level controls how much a source is amplified and is sometimes labeled as the Mic Gain Trim, Mic Preamp, Input Preamp, Trim, Preamp, or Gain.

A signal that's been patched into a microphone input has entered the mixer before the preamp. The preamp needs to receive a signal that is at mic level. Mic level (typically 30–60 dB below line level) is what we call the strength of the signal that comes out of the mic as it hears your music. A mic level signal must be amplified to a signal strength that the mixer wants. Mixers work at line level so a mic level signal needs to be amplified by the preamp to line level before it gets to the rest of the signal path.

Best results are usually achieved when the preamp doesn't need to be turned all the way up. A preamp circuit usually re-circulates the signal back through itself to amplify. This process can add noise, then amplify that noise, then amplify that noise, etc. So, use as little preamplification as possible to achieve sufficient line level.

Some mixers have an LED (light-emitting diode, or red light) next to the preamp control. This is a peak level indicator and is used to indicate peak signal strength that either is or is getting close to overdriving the input. The proper way to adjust the preamp control is to turn it up until the peak LED is blinking occasionally, then decrease the preamp level slightly. It's usually okay if the peak LED blinks a few times during a recording.

Many modern mixers have very clean and transparent input preamps with ample headroom—headroom, in any circuit, is the operational range between normal and maximum signal level. These mixers rarely utilize a peak LED at the input stage to help set the preamp level. In this case, the channel fader and master stereo are optimized at unity gain. (Unity gain is the state where a circuit outputs the same level it receives at its input.) When the channel fader is set at unity (U) the preamp level is adjusted to produce the proper level for recording or reinforcement.

Adjusting Channel Gain

There are two basic methods to adjust initial gain settings.

1. The channel on the left demonstrates the use of channel peak LED to adjust the input level. With this method, while the source is active, turn the trim up until the peak LED blinks, then back the trim off slightly.

2. The channel on the right demonstrates a unity setting on the channel fader. Set the fader to unity and then adjust the trim for the proper mix level. Most boards that use this system offer a means to meter the input signal. Many mixers display the channel level on the main left-right meter when the channel solo button is selected.

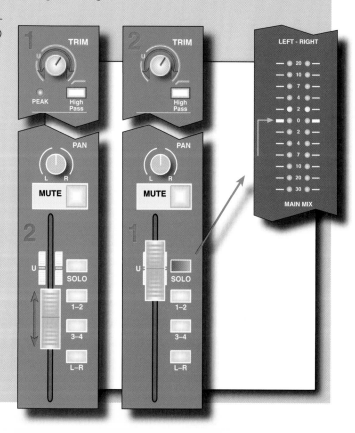

Attenuator

It's a fact that sometimes the signal that comes from a microphone or instrument into the board is too strong for the preamp stage of your mixer. This can happen when miking a very loud instrument, like a drum or electric guitar amp, or when accepting the DI of a guitar, sound module, or bass with particularly strong output levels. Some microphones produce a stronger signal than others. This is a particular problem when miking drums or loud guitar and bass amplification systems. If the signal is too strong going into the preamp, then there will be unacceptable distortion. When this happens at the input, there's no fixing it later.

This situation requires the use of an attenuator, also called a pad. This is almost always found at the top of each channel by the preamp level control. Sometimes, especially on condenser microphones there is a pad between the mic capsule and the microphone circuitry. Try this attenuator before using the mixer attenuator.

An attenuator restricts the flow of signal into the preamp by a measured amount or, in some cases, by a variable amount. Most attenuators include 10, 20 or 30 dB pads, which are labeled −10 dB, −20 dB, or −30 dB. Listen to Audio Example 4-1 to hear the sound of an overdriven input. This example would sound clean and clear if only the attenuator switch were set correctly!

Video Example 4-1

Demonstration of Trim Adjustment

Audio Example 4-1

The Overdriven Input

If there's noticeable distortion from a sound source, even if the preamp is turned down, use the pad. Start with the least amount of pad available first. If distortion disappears, all is well. If there's still distortion, try more attenuation.

Once the distortion is gone, use the preamp level control to attain sufficient input level. Listen to Audio Example 4-2 to hear the dramatic difference this adjustment can make in the clarity of an audio signal.

Audio Example 4-2
Attenuator Adjustment

Again, if the input stage of your mixer has a red peak LED by the input level control, it's desirable to turn the input up until the peak LED blinks occasionally, then back the level off slightly. This way we know we have the signal coming into the mixer as hot as possible without distortion. This is good.

Ideally, we'll always record electronic instruments with their output at maximum going into the board. This procedure results in the best possible signal-to-noise (S/N) ratio and provides a more surefire way to get the instrument back to its original level for a punch-in or retake.

If you don't have an attenuator and if you are recording from an instrument like bass, keyboard or guitar through a direct box, you can turn the output of the instrument down slightly to keep from overdriving the input preamp. Be sure to mark or notate the position of the instrument's controls (especially volume) so you can duplicate levels for a future punch-in or retake.

Meters

We must use meters to tell how much signal is getting to the console, recorders, outboard gear, etc. There are two different types of meters

Dynamic Range/Signal-to-Noise Ratio

When addressing sonic quality and integrity we often use two terms: dynamic range and signal-to-noise ratio. In the simplest of terms, dynamic range is the distance, in decibels, from the softest sound to the loudest sound in any audio signal. The signal-to-noise ratio (abbreviated S/N ratio or SNR) simply specifies the distance, in decibels, from the noise floor to the loudest sound in an audio signal.

Mathematically, the S/N ratio is expressed as 20 times the base-10 logarithm of the amplitude ratio, or 10 times the logarithm of the power ratio. Don't worry too much about the math, for right now—simply keep in mind that we should always strive to accurately capture the full dynamic range of any source and, to accomplish this, our signal-to-noise ratio should match or exceed the dynamic range of the source.

Practically speaking, a signal with full amplitude exceeding the noise floor by 100 dB is said to have a S/N ratio of 100 dB—higher is always better. An audio source with 100 dB maximum level and a 20 dB minimum level is said to have a dynamic range of 80 dB.

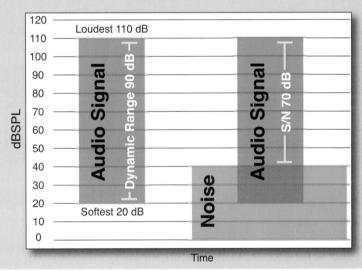

in common use today: the Volume Unit (VU) meter and the Peak Program Meter (PPM).

Volume Unit (VU)

In the modern recording world, VU meters are the least common type of meter. They're very common in application to analog recording. VU stands for Volume Unit. This meter, with an average rise and fall time of about .3 seconds, reads average signal levels, not peak levels or fast attacks. A VU meter has a needle that moves across a scale from about −20 VU up to about +5 VU. The act of moving the needle's physical mass across the VU scale keeps this meter from being able to follow fast attacks. When recording to analog tape the VU meter is a very efficient way to meter signal strength. Part of the advantage of analog audio is the sound of the audio that's been recorded very hot. Tape distortion softens a sound and often helps it blend into the mix in an appealing way. Using peak meters to measure signal strength in the analog domain usually results in a recording that is conservative in level and abundant in noise.

The VU meter enjoys continued popularity in the broadcast world, since its readings correspond closely to the perceived loudness of speech signals.

VU meters are commonly used in outboard equipment to monitor input and output strength, as well as parameters like gain reduction, and other dynamic controls. In these applications they are easy to read and provide an excellent visual representation of average signal levels.

Peak Program Meters (PPM)

Peak program meters accurately meter fast attacks from percussive instruments. Nearly instantaneous, sharp attacks, like those from any metal or hard wood instrument that is struck by a hard stick or mallet, are called transients. Peak meters contain a series of small lights that turn on immediately in response to a predetermined voltage. Since there's no movement of a physical mass (like the VU meter's needle), peak meters are ideal for accurately indicating transients.

Since the reaction of the meter to an incoming signal is electronic, rather than physical, the speed of the meter is adjustable by simply adjusting the speed of the electronic rise and release. Typically, a PPM has a potential rise time of about 10 milliseconds and a fall time potential of about 4 seconds.

Many peak program meters are selectable between peak and average readings. Average signal level readings are still valuable, especially considering that average signal strength offers a close correlation to the loudness of speech signals.

Peak and VU Meters

Zero, on a peak meter, registers maximum level; zero on a VU measures optimum average level, with several dB headroom before maximum level is attained. There is an art to using a VU meter, where your knowledge and insight to the operational characteristic influence level assessment. Peak meters are typically used for digital metering; they provide black and white assessment of level—you've reached overload or you haven't. Many engineers prefer to meter levels, especially mixdown levels, on both peak and VU meters. VU meters equate more closely to actual loudness. If you control peak levels and maintain strong VU levels throughout, you can be assured that your mix is strong and clean.

Typically, digital peak meters and VU meters are compared using a 1 kHz tone. Originally, 0 VU when fed by the identical 1 kHz tone, was equated to –18 on the digital peak meter. This provided plenty of headroom for transients and overloads—it also produced very conservative recording levels. As engineers began to realize that full digital level meant full vertical resolution, some manufacturers started to equate zero VU to –12 Peak—still allowing headroom for transients while providing better digital resolution. This comparison is typically viable, although, when metering audio signals digitally, optimize audio resolution by achieving maximum level without overload.

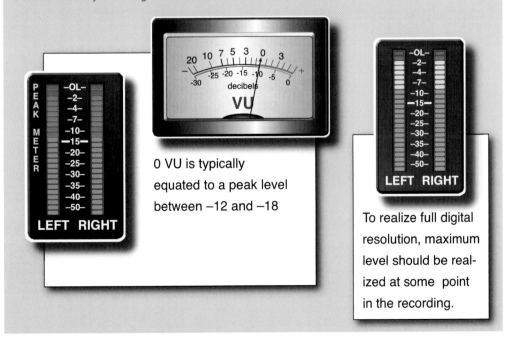

0 VU is typically equated to a peak level between –12 and –18

To realize full digital resolution, maximum level should be realized at some point in the recording.

Peak meters are necessary for recording digitally, since our primary goal, using a digital recorder, is to not record above a certain level with any signal. When recording digitally, always try to obtain the highest meter reading without going past 0. If digital recordings are made with levels too low, the full resolution of the digital recording process isn't realized. Low-level digital recordings sound grainy and harsh.

Adjusting Record Levels for Transients

A transient attack is the percussive attack present in all percussion instruments when one hard surface is struck with a hard stick, mallet or beater (cymbals, tambourine, cowbell, claves, guiro, shakers, maracas, etc.). Transient attacks are also a consideration when recording acoustic guitar (especially steel string played with a pick) or acoustic piano.

When recording instruments that contain transients and metering with a standard VU meter, adjust levels so that the loudest part of the track registers between −9 VU and −7 VU. This approach results in much more accurate and clean percussive type tracks. The transient is usually at least 9 VU hotter than the average level, so when the standard VU meter reads −9 VU the tape is probably seeing 0 VU. If you meter 0 VU on a transient, the tape might see +9 VU!

A peak LED is normally just one red light that comes on when the signal is about to over saturate tape, overdrive a circuit, or exceed maximum digital level.

It's usually okay for the peak LED that lives in one corner of a VU meter to blink occasionally, but if it's on continuously, back the level off until it blinks less.

When a peak LED comes on, it means that, even though the VU is registering well within acceptable limits, the actual level that's reaching tape is getting pretty hot.

In a mix, if the average or VU level is conservative but the peak LEDs are always on, there's probably a percussion instrument in your mix that's too loud, and even if it doesn't sound too loud on your system, it'll probably sound too loud on other systems.

When recording most instruments using a VU meter, adjust the recording level so that VU meters read 0 VU to +2 VU at the strongest parts of the track. For percussive instruments that have transient attacks, also called transient peaks, the VU meter should read around –9 VU to –7 VU at the peaks.

As a rule, meter analog signals with VU meters and meter digital signals with peak program meters.

Video Example 4-2

VU and Peak Meter From the Same Sound Source

Phase

As we discovered in Chapter 1, if two signals are electronically out of phase their waveforms are mirror images of each other. The crest of one wave happens simultaneously with the identical trough of the other wave. When this happens, there is phase cancellation—in other words, no signal. If two waveforms are in phase, they crest and trough together. This results in a doubling of the amount of energy from that waveform, or twice the amount of air being moved.

When phase problems occur, they're typically a result of two basic scenarios:

+ An incorrectly wired microphone, or balanced line cable

+ Multiple microphones in the same acoustic space, recorded at the same time, and spaced so that undesirable phase interactions occur as the same sound arrives at the different mics in destructive phase relations

This problem doesn't show up as much in a stereo mix, but anytime your mix is played in mono or anytime you are combining multiple microphones to the mix center, this can be the worst problem of all. To hear the effect of combining a sound with itself in and out of phase, listen to the guitar in Audio Example 4-3.

At the beginning of Audio Example 4-3 the original track is playing into one channel of the mixer. Next, the signal is split and run into another channel of the mixer. Notice the volume increase as the two channels are combined. Finally, the Audio Example shows the sound difference as the phase is reversed on the second track. The tracks combined are obviously thin and reduced in level. Imagine if that happened to the guitar track in a mix as it was played on mono through your sound system at a gig or on AM radio.

Audio Examples 4-3

Phase Reversal

The nature of combining sounds dictates that there is always phase interaction. We wouldn't want to hinder that because good phase interaction gives our music depth and richness. However, we do want to be particularly aware of phase interactions that can have an adverse effect on the quality of our music.

If your mixer has a phase switch on each channel, it's probably at the top of the channel by the preamp and attenuator controls. Its purpose is to help compensate for phase interaction problems. For practical use, listen to your mixes in mono. If you notice that too many instruments get softer, disappear or just seem to sound funny in mono, then there's probably a phase problem between some of the tracks. Change the phase of some of the tracks that might be combining in a problematic way until the mix sounds full and smooth in mono.

Short delay times, chorus and phasing effects can also cause these kinds of problems in mono, so you might also need to change some delay times to help even things out. There will be more about this when we cover mixdown. Once you've located and solved the phase problems, your mix will sound just as good in stereo, and you'll be ready for television or AM radio.

It's a good idea to be checking for phase problems when recording tracks to the multitrack. Some mixers that have phase reversal switches have them operable only on the mic inputs and not on the tape inputs. Therefore, they're unavailable during mixdown.

Input Level Comparison

These initial variables (preamp, attenuator, meters, and phase) are very important points for us to deal with. Any good engineer has a solid grasp of these crucial parts of the signal path. These are the basics; you'll continually return to them for clean, quality, professional recordings.

As reinforcement of the importance of proper adjustment of the input stage of your mixer, listen to Audio Examples 4-4, 4-5, and 4-6. If your signal isn't clean and accurate at the input stage, it won't be clean and accurate anywhere.

Audio Example 4-4

Proper Input Levels

Audio Example 4-5

Low Input Levels Resulting in a Noisy Mix

Audio Example 4-6

High Input Levels Causing Distortion

We must have proper levels coming into the mixer before we can even begin to set levels to tape. Any distortion here is magnified at each point. Any noise that exists here is magnified at each point. Listen to the effects of improper level adjustment at the input. Audio Examples 4-5, 4-6 and 4-7 use the same song, the same mixer and the same tracks with different input levels. All three of these audio examples are recorded at the same mixdown level; the only variable is the input trim level.

Notice in Audio Example 4-5 the sound is clean and strong. This was recorded with the input levels set properly. In Audio Example 4-5, the input level is set very low. When this happens the levels at the end of the signal path must be elevated unnaturally in order to achieve proper mixdown levels. Along with raising levels at the final stages of the signal path comes the noise that inherently resides in the mixer circuitry.

Audio Example 4-6 is simply too hot coming into the signal path. The distortion here happens immediately. There's no way to fix the problem when the audio is distorted at the input stage.

Channel Insert

Most modern mixers have what is called a channel insert. This is the point where a piece of outboard signal processing can be plugged into the signal path on each individual channel. If your mixer has inserts, they're probably directly above or below the microphone inputs.

A channel insert lets you access only one channel at a time and is used to include a signal processor in the signal path of that specific channel.

Channel Insert

Many mixers have a channel insert. This is the point where an outboard signal processor can be plugged into the signal path. If your mixer has inputs, they're probably directly above or below the mic inputs.

A channel insert will have a send that sends the signal, usually as it comes out of the preamp, to the processor. The output of the signal processor is then patched into the return of the channel insert. This completes the signal path. The signal then continues on its way through the EQ circuit and on through the rest of its path.

The processor you insert becomes a permanent part of the signal path from that point on. An insert is especially useful when using a compressor, gate, or other dynamic processor.

A channel insert utilizes a send to send the signal (usually as it comes out of the preamp) to the signal processor. The signal processor output is then patched into the return of the channel insert. This completes the signal path, and the signal typically continues on its way through the EQ circuit and on through the rest of its path.

A channel insert and an effects bus are similar in that they can both deal with signal processing. An insert affects one channel only. Inserts are ideal for patching dynamics processors, like compressors, limiters and gates, into a signal path.

Three Common Types of Channel Inserts

1. A Simple Send and Return with Separate 1/4" jacks

Inside the mixer, the send is normally connected to the return when no plugs are in the jacks. With this sort of setup, the send and return are said to be normalled, because they are normally connected together. That connection can be interrupted by inserting a plug into one or both of the jacks.

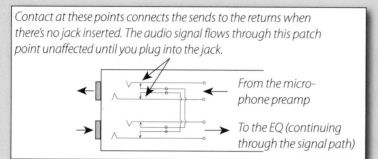

Contact at these points connects the sends to the returns when there's no jack inserted. The audio signal flows through this patch point unaffected until you plug into the jack.

From the micro-phone preamp

To the EQ (continuing through the signal path)

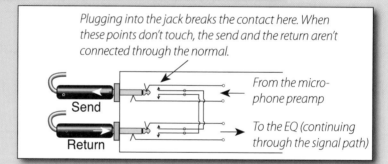

Plugging into the jack breaks the contact here. When these points don't touch, the send and the return aren't connected through the normal.

Send

Return

From the micro-phone preamp

To the EQ (continuing through the signal path)

2. Jumpered Sends and Returns

This method also uses separate send and return jacks (usually RCA phono), but instead of being normalled internally, the send is connected to the return using a simple jumper plug. The send and return are only connected when the jumper is plugged into both RCA jacks at once. If this jumper is removed, you won't hear the signal. When outboard processing is needed, simply remove the jumper, patch the send to the input of the processor and then patch the processor output to the return.

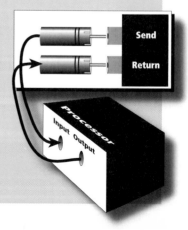

Send

Return

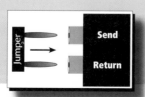

Jumper

Send

Return

Three Common Types of Channel Inserts (cont.)

3. The Single Insert Jack

Another common type of insert uses a single insert jack. To utilize this type of insert, you must use a special Y cable, like the one below (male tip-ring-sleeve stereo 1/4" phone plug to two female tip-sleeve mono 1/4" phone jacks).

Plug the male stereo phone plug into the insert. Next, use a line cable to connect one of the female mono connectors to the processor input, and patch the output of the processor into the other female mono connector. You might need to experiment to determine which of the mono connectors is the send and which is the return. Once everything is working, label the Y cable so it will be easy to use next time you need it.

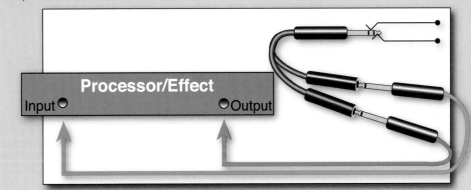

Effects Bus

An effects bus (like aux 1 or aux 2) lets you send a mix from the bus to an effect (typically outside the mixer but often simply routed internally to an effect, headphones, etc.), leaving the master mix on the input faders without effects. The output of the effect is then plugged into the effects returns or open channels on the mixer. This is good for reverbs and multi-effects processors.

When we discuss the input faders as a group, we're talking about a bus. The term bus is confusing to many, but the basic concept of a bus is simple—and very important to understand. A bus usually refers to a row of faders or knobs.

If you think about a city bus, you know that it has a point of origin (one bus depot) and a destination (another depot), and you know that it picks up passengers and delivers them to their destination. That's exactly what a bus on a mixer does. For example, in mixdown the faders bus has a point of origin (the recorded tracks) and a destination (the mixdown recorder). Its passengers are the different tracks from the multitrack. Not all tracks (passengers) necessarily get on the bus, but whoever rides goes to the same destination.

Most mixers also have auxiliary buses, or effects buses). Aux buses (also called cue sends, effects sends, or monitor sends) operate in the same way as the faders bus. An aux bus (another complete set of knobs or faders) might have its point of origin at the multitrack or the mic/line inputs. It picks up its own set of the available passengers (tracks) and takes them to their own destination (usually an effects unit or the headphones).

When a bus is used with an effect, like a reverb, delay, or multi-effects processor, the individual controls on the bus are called effects sends because they're sending different instruments or tracks to the effects unit on this bus. The entire bus is also called a send.

Return is a term that goes with send. The send sends the musical ingredients to the reverb or effect. The return accepts the output of the reverb or effect as it returns to the mix.

Managing the Signal Path

This section covers input faders, gain structure, buses, track assignments, pan, solo, and mute.

Input Faders

Once everything is set properly at the preamp, use the input faders to set the recording level to tape, or simply use them to adjust monitor levels.

Mixing live sound is different than recording. In a live mix, the main channel faders are used to set the mix volumes for each channel. In a recording session these faders might be used during tracking to set the recording level, with another knob or fader controlling the actual mix. On the other hand, there might be another knob or fader that adjusts the level to the recorder with the main channel fader controlling the mix.

Many recording consoles provide you the flexibility to configure the layout according to your preference. Whichever way you choose to work, for our purposes right now, it's important that you understand this fundamental difference between a live mixer and a recording mixer.

Input Faders

Monitor Level controls receive signals from the multitrack output. When recording tracks to the multitrack, adjust the record levels with the Main Fader and adjust the listening volumes with the Monitor Level controls.

Some recording mixers offer level control via a rotary knob; some via a fader. No matter which configuration, the primary difference between a live sound console and a recording console is this concept, in which the input channel adjusts the recording level, yet the multitrack might, or night not, return to the same or a different channel. You must constantly keep the recorder track in mind for monitoring purposes.

Pre and Post

Aux buses often include a switch that chooses whether each individual point in the bus hears the signal before it gets to the EQ and fader (indicated by the word pre) or after the EQ and fader (indicated by the word post).

Selecting Pre lets you set up a mix that's totally separate from the input faders and EQ. This is good for headphone sends. Once the headphone mix is good for the musicians, it's best to leave it set. You don't want changes you make for your listening purposes to change the musicians' mix in the phones.

Selecting Post is good for effects sends. A bus used for reverb sends works best when the send to the reverb decreases as the instrument or voice fader is turned down. Post sends are perfect for this application since the send is after the fader. As the fader is decreased, so is the send to the reverb, maintaining a constant balance between the dry and affected sounds. If a Pre send is used for reverb, the channel fader can be off, but the send to the reverb is still on. When your channel fader is down, the reverb return can still be heard, loud and clear.

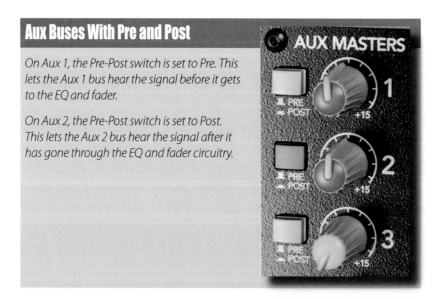

Aux Buses With Pre and Post

On Aux 1, the Pre-Post switch is set to Pre. This lets the Aux 1 bus hear the signal before it gets to the EQ and fader.

On Aux 2, the Pre-Post switch is set to Post. This lets the Aux 2 bus hear the signal after it has gone through the EQ and fader circuitry.

Using the Aux Bus

Imagine there's a guitar on track 4, and it's turned up in the mix. We hear the guitar clean and dry. Dry means the sound is heard without effect. The guitar in Audio Example 4-7 is dry.

Audio Example 4-7

Dry Guitar

If the output of aux bus 1 is patched into a reverberation input, and the aux 1 send is turned up at channel 4, we should see a reading at the input meter of the reverb when the recorder is rolling and the track is playing. This indicates that we have a successful send to the reverb.

The reverb can't be heard until we patch the output of the reverb into either an available, unused channel of the mixer or into a dedicated effects return. If your mixer has specific effects returns, it's often helpful to think of these returns as simply one or more extra channels on your mixer.

Once the effects outputs are patched into the returns, raise the return levels on the mixer to hear the reverb coming into the mix. Find the adjustment on your reverb that says wet/dry. The signal coming from the reverb should be 100 percent wet. That means it's putting out only reverberated sound and none of the dry sound. Maintain separate control of the dry track. Get the reverberated sound only from the completely wet returns. With separate wet and dry control, you can blend the sounds during mixdown to produce just the right sonic blend. Listen to Audio Examples 4-8, 4-9 and 4-10 to hear the dry and wet sounds being blended in the mix.

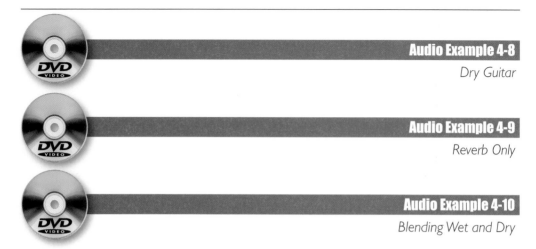

Audio Example 4-8
Dry Guitar

Audio Example 4-9
Reverb Only

Audio Example 4-10
Blending Wet and Dry

The Headphone Bus

If your mixer has a headphone bus, or if you're using an auxiliary bus to send a signal to the headphones, patch the output of that bus into a headphone amplifier. You'll hear the mix you've sent to the headphone amp (from the headphone bus) when you plug headphones into the outputs of the headphone amp. The individual auxiliary buses on a mixer are sometimes powered just enough to run headphones; however, a good headphone amplifier provides ample power while typically offering multiple outputs with level control for recording groups of musicians.

If there's an output on your mixer labeled Headphones, it's probably powered, and you won't need a headphone amp. If you're patching this output into an amp, the powered send has the potential to overdrive the input. The resulting sound will be distorted and unsatisfactory. If the headphone output is minimally powered, you might be able to patch it into a separate headphone amp, but you must be careful to keep the headphone output level low.

The headphone output often derives its signal from the main faders. In some cases, there's a selector to let you listen to different buses.

Track Assignment

Assigning

The track assignment section, also called the bus assign section or switching matrix, is used to send whatever is received at the input of the mixer (mic, instrument, or tape) to any one or a combination of output buses. These bus outputs are normally connected to the inputs of the multitrack.

A 4-bus board provides you the option of sending your signal to any one or more of the four main outputs of the mixer that are connected to the multitrack recorder inputs. In the case that your multitrack recorder has more tracks than your mixer has buses, each bus is split to two or three tracks in multiples of the number of buses. For example, a 4-bus mixer connected to a 16-track multitrack splits bus one to tracks 1, 5, 9, and 13. Bus two splits to tracks 2, 6, 10, and 14. Bus 3 splits to tracks 3, 7, 11, and 15. Bus 4 splits to tracks 4, 8, 12, and 16.

This bus splitting process is especially common on 4- and 8-bus mixers. Large format consoles typically have a bus output for each track on the multitrack. Consoles frequently provide 24 to 32 buses. This is very convenient when tracking a very large group, and where time is limited.

Summing

Track assignments can also be used to combine two or more outputs to one input.

Avoid patching the outputs of two or more instruments (or other devices) together through a Y cable into one input. This typically over-drives and distorts the input. Anytime you sum (combine) multiple outputs to one input, use a circuit like the track assignment circuit on your mixer. This is designed specifically to maintain proper impedance and signal strength for its destination input. This type of circuit is also

Assigning Channels to Tracks

Channel 3 is switched to LINE
to monitor recorder

Channel 15 is switched to MIC
to send to the recorder

Even though channel 15 sends
signal, channel 3 monitors
the signal

Channel 15 assigned to
recorder track 3

Output 3 sends
level to recorder

called a combining bus, combining matrix, summing bus, summing matrix, switching matrix, track assignment bus or track assignment matrix.

Three Practical Applications for Splitting a Signal Using a Y

1. When sending a guitar to the direct input of a mixer and simultaneously to an amplifier: You can use a Y cable out of the guitar or the guitar effects setup

2. When sending a microphone signal to a live system and simultaneously to a recording system: A Y cable is also called a splitter; a splitter box usually has a snake that plugs into the recording board and outputs (or another snake) that plug into the live mixing board

3. When plugging the final output of a mixer into two or more mixdown recorders: If you're using a patch bay, all connections can be made with short, high quality patch cords for optimum signal transfer

Audio Examples 4-11, 4-12, and 4-13 demonstrate the sound of splitting the guitar signal with a Y cord straight out of the guitarist's effects. One side of the Y goes directly to the mixer through a direct box. The other side is sent to an amplifier. The amp is miked and the microphone is plugged into the mixer. This setup works well with a guitar, synth, drum machine or any other electronically generated sound source.

Audio Example 4-11 demonstrates the direct guitar sound.

Audio Example 4-11

Direct Guitar

Recording Direct and Miked

Most direct boxes have a Y built in. Input and Out to Amp are connected together to form an internal Y. The input also goes to the transformer on its way to the mixer. The Y lets you take the signal being fed into the Input of the DI and patch it out of the Out to Amp jack into any hi Z amplifier.

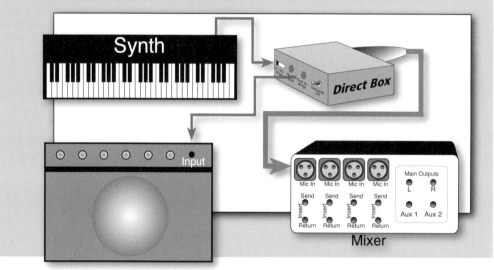

Listen to the miked amplifier in Audio Example 4-12.

Audio Example 4-12

The Miked Amp

We can combine the direct and miked guitar to one tape track with the track assignment bus. Listen to Audio Example 4-13 as the guitar sounds combine in different levels to create a new and interesting texture.

Audio Example 4-13

Combining Direct and Miked Signals

Pan

The pan control, sometimes called the pan pot (for panoramic potentiometer), is used to move a track in the stereo panorama. Sounds are positioned at any point in the left to right spectrum (between the left and right speakers). Some pan controls are either all the way left or all the way right with no position in between, but panning is usually infinitely sweepable from full left to full right or anywhere in between. Often the pan control is used for selecting odd or even track assignment on the multitrack bus assignments. Odd is left and even is right.

You can use the pan control along with the track assignment bus to combine multiple instruments, like several keyboards, to a stereo pair of recorder tracks. This can give you a very big sound while letting you get the most out of your equipment pool by conserving tracks and freeing up sound modules.

Listen to Audio Examples 4-14, 4-15, and 4-16. Three sounds are combined and panned around to create a unique sound that can't be gotten out of any single synth. A mixer lets you create a sound that's different from any other. Combining textures like this is called *layering* or sometimes *doubling*.

Audio Example 4-14 is synth sound A.

Audio Example 4-14
Synth Sound A

Listen to Audio Example 4-15 to hear synth sounds B and C combined with synth sound A.

Audio Example 4-15
Synth Sounds B and C

In Audio Example 4-16, synth sounds A, B, and C combine at different levels to become one unique and interesting sound.

Gain Structure

It's necessary to consider gain structure as we control different levels at different points in the signal path. Gain structure refers to the relative levels of the signal as it moves from the source to the destination. At each point where level changes are possible, you must monitor the signal strength and, if possible solo the signal.

We've already discussed the proper method for adjusting the input preamp level, and we've heard some examples of music recorded with the input stage too cold and too hot. These examples give an obvious demonstration of the importance of proper level adjustment at this primary stage. Each stage with user-controlled levels carries its own importance to the integrity of your signal. Ideally, you'll be able to adjust each stage to be as hot as possible, with minimal distortion.

Some mixers have a suggested unity setting for input faders and track assignment bus faders. They are usually indicated by a grayed area near the top of the fader's throw or numerically by a zero indication. Try placing the input and track assignment bus faders to their ideal settings. Then adjust the input preamp for proper recording level. This is a safe approach and works well much of the time.

Experiment with different approaches to find what works best with your setup. No approach works every time, so remember to trust your ears. If your sound is clean and punchy but the settings don't seem to be by the book, you're better off than if you have textbook settings on your mixer with substandard sound.

Confidence in your control of the gain structure can take time and experience, so start practicing. See what happens when you try a new approach.

If you adjust the input level properly, if the input fader is somewhere close to the ideal setting, and if the track assign bus/record level fader is also close to the ideal, all should be well. If one or more of these settings is abnormally high or low, you might have a problem with your gain structure.

Experiment with different approaches to find what works best with your setup. Remember to trust your ears. If your sound is clean and punchy but the settings don't seem to be by the book, that's better than having a textbook setting on your mixer and a substandard sound.

Potential Problems

If the input level is abnormally high (even if the signal isn't noticeably distorted), the input fader and/or track bus fader might be abnormally low. Faders work more smoothly and are easier to control in the upper part of the fader throw. When the fader is abnormally low, it's much more difficult to fade an instrument down or to fine-tune the record levels or monitor levels.

If the preamp level is destructively high, the signal will overdrive the mixer and the integrity of the entire signal path will be jeopardized. The preamp adjustment is very important. An improper setting here will result in surefire failure.

If the preamp level is abnormally low, the input fader and/or the track bus fader might be abnormally high. When this happens, the inherent noise that resides in your mixer is turned up further than it needs to be. Therefore, we end up with more noise in relation to signal (an undesirable signal-to-noise ratio). This is bad.

Bouncing Analog and DTR Tracks

- *Notice tracks 1, 2, and 3 are set to Tape on the Mic-Tape selector.*

- *Notice channels 1, 2, and 3 are assigned to tracks 7 and 8, and a mix of the three instruments is set up and panned. This mix is what will be recorded onto tracks 7 and 8.*

- *The output buses, 1 through 8, are connected to the recorder inputs 1 through 8. Often these outputs are split to multiple groups—1 through 8, 9 though 16, 17 through 24, etc. Notice 7 and 8 are up, sending level to the recorder.*

- *The recorder is monitored through channels 7 and 8. Notice that the only channels assigned to the LEFT-RIGHT bus are channels 7 and 8.*

- *With this setup, simply set the recorder tracks 7 and 8 to record-ready, then press play and record.*

Bouncing Tracks

In today's recording world, there are certain topics that apply primarily to analog recording and other topics that apply to the digital realm. Combining several tracks through a summing bus to one or two other tracks, referred to as bouncing or ping-ponging, is often necessary in the analog domain in order to clear out tracks for more musical ingredients—typically backing vocals or solo overdubs.

This procedure is common in the realm of analog multitrack recording and also when incorporating the use of Modular Digital Multitrack recorders like the Alesis ADAT or the Tascam DA-88. Given the flexibility of computer- and workstation-based multitracking in digital domain, bouncing tracks has become less important. Using software-based recording systems, it's easy to record several tracks, then route them all to the same output(s) for simple control. However, the bounce provides convenience and extends power in either the analog or digital domain.

Analog and Digital Tape-Based Recorders

Let's take a closer look at track assignments as they're used for bouncing tracks. Since the input of a mixer can be switched to listen to mic, line or tape, you select the input of two or three channels to listen to the tape. Once you've done this, for example, on tracks 1,2 and 3, you can assign these channels to track 4 at the track assignment bus.

Put track 4 into Record Ready and use the faders of 1,2 and 3 to set up the proper mix. Next, bounce those three tracks onto one by simply pressing play and record. Now start laying new parts down on 1, 2, and 3 as you listen to track 4.

Beware of bouncing to adjacent analog tracks. You run the risk of internal feedback of the tape machine anytime you bounce from a track to either track directly next to it. A lot depends on the alignment of your tape machine heads and the adjustment of your playback and record electronics. Digital multitrack formats like the ADAT and 8 mm systems have no problem bouncing to adjacent tracks.

If you have the option of choosing which tracks to bounce together, the best rule of thumb is to bounce an instrument with primarily low frequencies (like a bass) with an instrument that has primarily high frequencies (such as a tambourine). This lets you adjust their relative levels by adjusting EQ. Turning down the highs turns down the tambourine; turning down the lows turns down the bass. Listen to Audio Example 4-17 to hear a demonstration of this theory.

Bouncing Digital Workstation Tracks

Multiple benefits are provided by bouncing tracks digitally:

- *All processing power being used on the bounced tracks is released once the bounce is completed. The result of the bounce includes all plug-in effects, edits, crossfades, level changes, pans, automation, etc., across all selected tracks.*

- *The bounce is non-destructive to the original tracks. You can always go back and re-bounce if necessary.*

- *A stereo bounce of many tracks is much easier to handle than several individual tracks.*

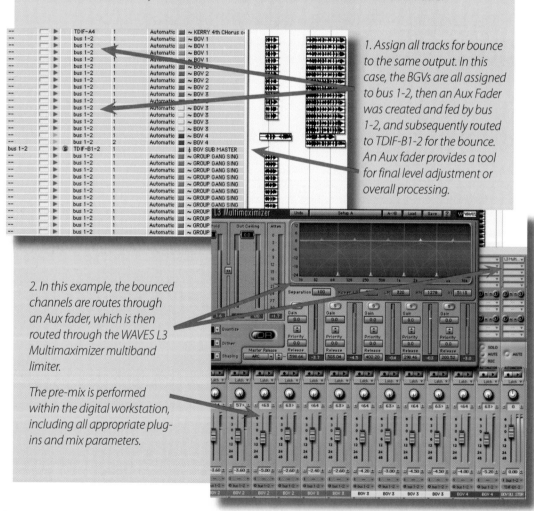

1. Assign all tracks for bounce to the same output. In this case, the BGVs are all assigned to bus 1-2, then an Aux Fader was created and fed by bus 1-2, and subsequently routed to TDIF-B1-2 for the bounce. An Aux fader provides a tool for final level adjustment or overall processing.

2. In this example, the bounced channels are routes through an Aux fader, which is then routed through the WAVES L3 Multimaximizer multiband limiter.

The pre-mix is performed within the digital workstation, including all appropriate plug-ins and mix parameters.

Bouncing Digital Workstation Tracks (cont.)

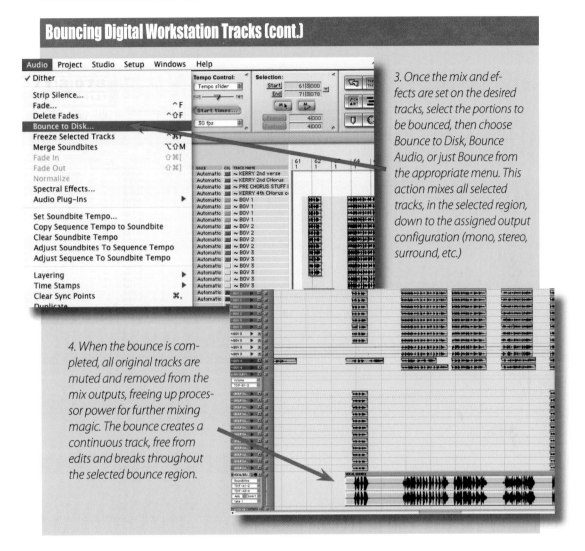

3. Once the mix and effects are set on the desired tracks, select the portions to be bounced, then choose Bounce to Disk, Bounce Audio, or just Bounce from the appropriate menu. This action mixes all selected tracks, in the selected region, down to the assigned output configuration (mono, stereo, surround, etc.)

4. When the bounce is completed, all original tracks are muted and removed from the mix outputs, freeing up processor power for further mixing magic. The bounce creates a continuous track, free from edits and breaks throughout the selected bounce region.

It's also very convenient to bounce submixes of large groups of tracks, like backing vocals.

Audio Example 4-17

Bouncing Multiple Instruments to One Track

Digital

Even in the digital realm, there are appropriate times for bouncing audio. If all your audio is mixed and shaped within the software package, the most efficient procedure for storing the mix is to bounce the audio, through a stereo or surround bus, to the hard drive. Most bounce options let you bounce in the format of your choice for playback on CD, DVD, etc.

There are also occasions during tracking where bouncing audio is appropriate. If you are on the verge of maxing out you computer processor, or if you're reaching the limit of your software's available tracks, simply bounce several tracks to a stereo pair. This will open more available processor power and tracks.

Since the digital bounce is typically non-destructive to the original tracks, bouncing is sometimes a matter of mix convenience more than anything. Many projects require several backing vocal tracks. Sometimes, for example, I've recorded 30 or more backing vocals. This becomes a logistical issue more than anything else. It is very convenient to bounce those tracks, as a stereo premix, to a pair of tracks.

Once the bounce is complete, simply turnoff the original tracks, releasing processing power, and turn on the new stereo bounce. This streamlines the rest of the tracking procedure because it is much easier to control two tracks than it is to control 30. If the premix isn't just right, the original tracks are still available for revised premix at a later date. Whereas, an analog bounce is destructive, because you must erase over the original tracks to record more parts, the software bounce is much less risky because the original tracks aren't destroyed as the production unfolds.

Video Example 4-3

Bouncing Digital Workstation Tracks

Solo

A Solo button turns everything off except the soloed track. This lets you hear one track or instrument by itself, as if it were a solo. The solo function overrides the monitor signal. Listen as I press the Solo button on different tracks in Audio Example 4-18. You can also combine solos to hear a group of tracks together.

Audio Example 4-18

Soloing

This feature is very useful in evaluating a track for cleanliness of signal and quality of sound. It's often impossible to tell what's really going on with a track when listening to it in the context of the rest of the arrangement.

There are three main types of soloing: PFL, AFL, and MIXDOWN.

PFL (Pre Fader Listen)

PFL stands for Pre Fader Listen. The PFL button solos a channel immediately before the fader. This provides an accurate picture of how a particular channel is sounding just as it's going into your mix or just before it gets to the multitrack. The position of the channel fader has no affect on the PFL solo since the signal is tapped prior to its arrival at the fader. Often, the PFL solo isn't affected by EQ or pan settings either.

PFL is usually the best way to verify signal integrity since it is closest to the source. If the signal is clean at the PFL position and unsatisfactory at the channel fader, a patching or console problem is likely.

The PFL solo button doesn't affect the main outputs, aux sends, or mixdown sends. Since it is non-destructive to the mix output the PFL solo provides an excellent way to quickly verify the signal on a specific channel. In the broadcast industry, utilizing the PFL is sometimes referred to as *cueing*.

AFL (After Fader Listen)

The AFL solo is, as its name indicates, affected by the fader position. The signal is soloed immediately after it leaves the fader and, in addition, is typically affected by the EQ and pan and mute settings. AFL provides a convenient way to monitor a group of related tracks, by themselves, with all their level, EQ, and pan positions as they sound in the mix. A mixer with only one solo button is typically soloing AFL. AFL is sometimes called "solo in place" since it retains pan positioning.

MIXDOWN Solo

The MIXDOWN solo feature is very similar to the AFL. It soles just prior to entering the mixdown bus. All panning, EQ, inserts, mutes are in effect, just like most AFL solo functions.

MIXDOWN solo is typically incorporated in console automation. With a computer-assisted mixdown, a mixdown solo button actually writes the solo into automation data. This is a very convenient feature, especially in genre where musical and textural breakdowns are common.

Mutes

A Mute button is an off button. A channel mute turns the channel off. Use the mutes instead of the faders to turn a channel down, especially when setting up a mix or setting levels for a tracking session. Beginning recordists often pull the faders down instead of using the mutes. Once you have a channel level set in relation to the other channels, you'll save time by simply muting and unmuting. The levels will remain the same, and you'll avoid continual rebalancing.

The Equalizer

The equalizer or EQ section is usually located at about the center of each channel and is definitely one of the most important sections of the mixer. EQ is also called tone control; highs and lows; or highs, mids and lows. Onboard EQ typically has an in/out or bypass button. With the button set to in, your signal goes through the EQ. With the button set to out or bypass, the EQ circuitry is not in the signal path. If you're not using EQ, it is best to bypass the circuit rather than just set all of the controls to flat (no boost and no cut). Anytime you bypass a circuit, you eliminate one more possibility for coloration or distortion.

From a purist's standpoint, EQ is to be used sparingly, if at all. Before you use EQ, use the best mic choice and technique. Be sure the instrument you're miking sounds its best. Trying to mike a poorly tuned drum can be a nightmare. It's a fact that you can get wonderful sounds with just the right mic in just the right place on just the right instrument. That's the ideal.

From a practical standpoint, there are many situations where using EQ is the only way to a great sound on time and on budget. This is especially true if you don't own a wide array of mics. During mixdown, proper use of EQ is fundamental to an outstanding mix.

Proper control of each instrument's unique tone (also called its timbre) is one of the most musical uses of the mixer, so let's look more closely at equalization. There are several different types of EQ on the hundreds of different mixers available. What we want to look at are some basic principles that are common to all kinds of mixers, as well as outboard equalizers.

We use EQ for two different purposes: to get rid of (cut) part of the tone that we don't want and to enhance (boost) some part of the tone that we do want. Boosting and cutting frequency ranges are both

Equalization Curve - Bandwidth

Boosting or cutting a particular frequency also boosts or cuts the frequencies nearby. If you boost 500 Hz on an equalizer, 500 Hz is the center point of a curve being boosted. Keep in mind that a substantial range of frequencies might be boosted along with the center point of the curve. The exact range of frequencies boosted is dependent upon the shape of the curve.

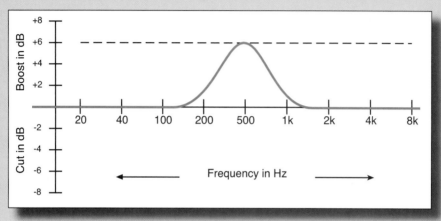

very important. A young recordist typically reaches for equalization to add highs or lows, but rarely listens to a sound to critically locate a frequency range to cut.

Hertz

Boosting and cutting at a specified frequency number on any equalizer (for example, 100 Hz) alters more than just one frequency. It alters a frequency band that is sometimes adjustable in width. So, when we say, "Boost the bass guitar track at 100 Hz," we're really indicating a frequency range with its center at 100 Hz.

The ability to hear the effect of isolating these frequency bands provides a point of reference from which to work. Try to learn the sound of each frequency band and the number of Hertz that goes with that sound.

To understand boosting or cutting a frequency, picture a curve with its center point at that frequency.

Listen to the effect that cutting and boosting certain frequencies has on Audio Examples 4-19 to 4-27.

Audio Example 4-19

Boost Then a cut at 60 Hz

Audio Example 4-20

Boost Then a Cut at 120 Hz

Audio Example 4-21

Boost Then a Cut at 240 Hz

Audio Example 4-22

Boost Then a Cut at 500 Hz

Audio Example 4-23

Boost Then a Cut at 1 kHz

Audio Example 4-24

Boost Then a Cut at 2 kHz

Audio Example 4-25

Boost Then a Cut at 4 kHz

Audio Example 4-26

Boost Then a Cut at 8 kHz

Audio Example 4-27

Boost Then a Cut at 16 kHz

Our goal in understanding and recognizing these frequencies is to be able to create sound pieces that fit together. The frequencies in Audio Examples 4-19 to 4-27 represent most of the center points for the sliders on a 10-band graphic EQ.

Video Example 4-4

Demonstration of Equalizer Changes on Various Sounds

If the guitar track a has a balance of the entire frequency range, it might sound great all by itself. If the bass track has a very broad-range sound with lots of highs and lows, it might sound great all by itself. If the keyboard track has a huge, broadband sound, it might sound great all by itself. However, when you put these instruments together in a song, they'll probably get in each other's way and cause problems for the overall mix.

Ideally, find the frequencies that are unnecessary on each track, cut those, then enhance, or boost, the frequency ranges you like. Keep the big picture in mind while selecting frequencies to cut or boost. Boost and cut different frequency ranges on the different instruments and fit the pieces together like a puzzle.

For instance, if the bass sounds muddy and needs to be cleaned up by cutting at about 250 Hz and if the high end of the bass could use a little attack at about 2500 Hz, that's great. When we EQ the electric guitar track, it's very possible that we could end up boosting the 250 Hz range to add punch. That works great because we've just filled the hole that we created in the bass EQ. Audio Example 4-28 demonstrates a bass recorded without EQ (flat).

Audio Example 4-28

Bass (Flat)

Listen to Audio Example 4-29 as I turn down a frequency with its center point at 250 Hz. It sounds much better because I've turned down the frequency range that typically clouds the sound.

Audio Example 4-29

Bass (Cut 250 Hz)

Audio Example 4-30 demonstrates a guitar recorded flat.

Audio Example 4-30

Guitar (Flat)

Audio Example 4-31 demonstrates the guitar with a boost at 250 Hz. This frequency is typical for adding punch to the guitar sound.

Audio Example 4-31

Guitar (Boost 250 Hz)

Audio Example 4-32 demonstrates the guitar and bass blending together. Notice how each part becomes more understandable as the EQ is inserted.

Audio Example 4-32

Guitar and Bass Together

In a mix, the lead or rhythm guitar doesn't generally need the lower frequencies below about 80 Hz. You can cut those frequencies substantially (if not completely), minimizing interference of the guitar's low end with the bass guitar.

If the guitar needs a little grind (edge, presence, etc.) in the high end, select from the 2 to 4 kHz range. Since you have already boosted 2.5 kHz on the bass guitar, the best choice is to boost 3.5 to 4 kHz on guitar. If these frequencies don't work well on the guitar, try shifting the bass high-end EQ slightly. Find different frequencies to boost on each instrument—frequencies that work well together and still sound good on the individual tracks. If you avoid equalizing each instrument at the same frequency, your song will sound smoother and it'll be easier to listen to on more systems.

Definition of Frequency Ranges

As I stated before, the range of frequencies that the human ear can hear is roughly from 20 Hz to 20 kHz. Individual response may vary, depending on age, climate and how many rock bands the ears' owner might have heard or played in. This broad frequency range is broken down into specific groups. It's necessary for us to know and recognize these ranges.

Listen to Audio Examples 4-33 to 4-43. I'll isolate these specific ranges.

Audio Example 4-33
Flat

Audio Example 4-34
Highs (Above 3.5 kHz)

Audio Example 4-35
Mids (250 Hz to 3.5 kHz)

Frequency Ranges

The range of frequencies that the human ear can hear is roughly from 20 Hz to 20 kHz. This broad frequency range is broken down into specific groups. It's necessary to know and recognize these ranges.

- *Highs - above 3.5 kHz*
- *Mids - between 250 Hz and 3.5 kHz*
- *Lows - below 250 Hz*

These are often broken into more specific categories:

- *Brilliance - above 6 kHz*
- *Presence - 3.5–6 kHz*
- *Upper midrange - 1.5–3.5 kHz*
- *Lower midrange - 250 Hz–1.5 kHz*
- *Bass - 60–250 Hz*
- *Sub-bass - below 60 Hz*

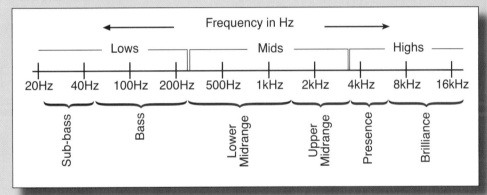

Lows (Below 250 Hz)

These are often broken down into more specific categories.

Listen to each of these more specific ranges.

Flat (Reference)

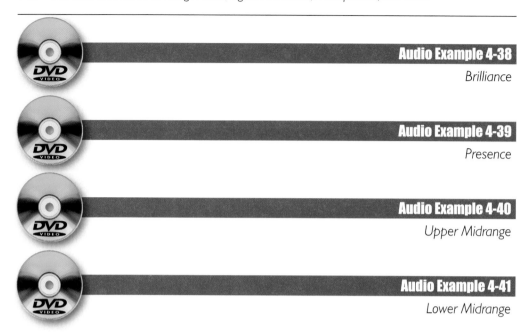

Audio Example 4-38

Brilliance

Audio Example 4-39

Presence

Audio Example 4-40

Upper Midrange

Audio Example 4-41

Lower Midrange

Bandwidth - The Q

Many equalizers let you control the width of the curve being manipulated. Notice the differing band-widths in this illustration. Refer to bandwidth in octaves or fractions of an octave.

- *Band #1 is about one octave wide.*
- *Band #2 is about two octaves wide.*
- *Band #3 is about half an octave wide.*

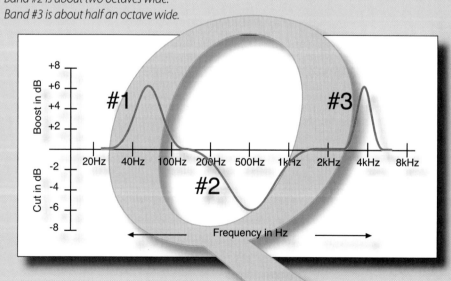

Selectable Frequencies

Two bands of EQ are available on each knob, enabling access to eight frequency bands. Pressing the Frequency Select button determines which frequency is boosted or cut. Each knob adjusts one frequency or the other, not both at the same time.

Freq. Select Button — Cut/Boost — 12kHz / 7.5kHz

Freq. Select Button — Cut/Boost — 4kHz / 1.8kHz

Freq. Select Button — Cut/Boost — 600Hz / 300Hz

Freq. Select Button — Cut/Boost — 150Hz / 80Hz

Audio Example 4-42

Bass

Audio Example 4-43

Sub-bass

Some of these ranges may be more or less audible on your system, though they're recorded at the same level. Even on the best system, these won't sound equally loud because of the uneven frequency response of the human ear.

Bandwidth

Bandwidth is simply the width, quantified in octaves, of a frequency spectrum. A human being hears a bandwidth of about 10 octaves—from 20 Hz to 20 kHz.

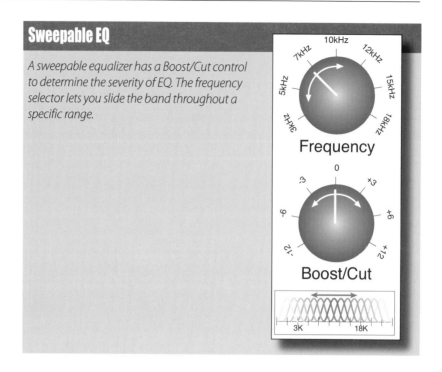

Sweepable EQ

A sweepable equalizer has a Boost/Cut control to determine the severity of EQ. The frequency selector lets you slide the band throughout a specific range.

Most equalizers contain controls for at least three bands, with each band about one octave wide. This means that the boost or cut is centered on the defining frequency but contains frequencies that extend 1/2 octave below the center point and 1/2 octave above the center point. A one-octave bandwidth is specific enough to enable us to get the job done but not so specific that we might create more problems than we eliminate. Bandwidth is sometimes referred to as the Q.

As the frequency band is raised or lowered, the frequencies on either side follow along in the overall shape of a bell curve centered on the given frequency. Bandwidth has to do with pinpointing how much of the frequency spectrum is being adjusted. A parametric equalizer is unique in that it has a bandwidth control.

A wide bandwidth (two or more octaves) is good for overall tone coloring. A narrow bandwidth (less than half an octave) is good for finding and fixing a problem.

Parametric EQ

The width of the selected frequency band is controlled by the Q adjustment (also called bandwidth). Curve A (below) is a very broad tone control. Curve B is a very specific pinpoint boost. The Q varies infinitely from its widest bandwidth to its narrowest. Frequency and Boost/Cut operate like the sweepable EQ.

Parametric equalization is the most flexible and powerful tone control.

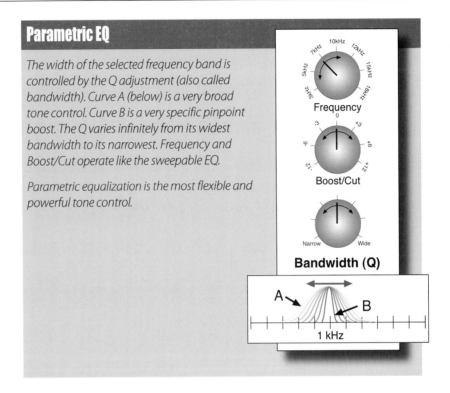

Sweepable EQ

A lot of mixers have sweepable EQ (also called semi parametric EQ). Sweepable EQ dramatically increases the flexibility of sound shaping. There are two controls per sweepable band:

1. A cut/boost control to turn the selected frequency up or down
2. A frequency selector that lets you sweep a certain range of frequencies

This is a very convenient and flexible EQ. With the frequency selector, you can zero in on the exact frequency you need to cut or boost. Often, the kick drum has one sweet spot where the lows are warm and rich or the attack on the guitar is at a very specific frequency. With sweepable EQ, you can set up a boost or cut, then dial in the frequency that breathes life into your music.

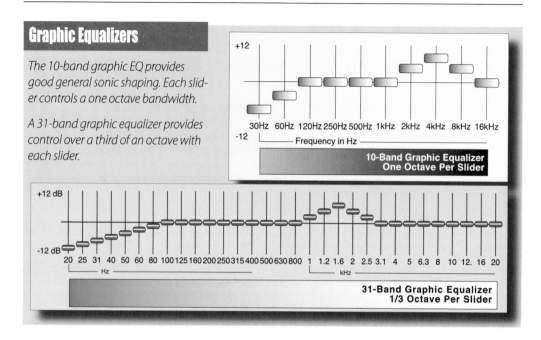

Graphic Equalizers

The 10-band graphic EQ provides good general sonic shaping. Each slider controls a one octave bandwidth.

A 31-band graphic equalizer provides control over a third of an octave with each slider.

Mixers that have sweepable EQ typically have three separate bands on each channel: one for highs, one for mids and one for lows. Sometimes the highs and lows are fixed-frequency equalizers but the mids are sweepable.

Parametric EQ

This is the most flexible type of EQ. It operates just like a sweepable EQ but gives you one other control: the bandwidth, or Q.

With the bandwidth control, you choose whether you're cutting or boosting a large range of frequencies or a very specific range of frequencies. For example, you might boost a four-octave band centered at 1000 Hz, or you might cut a very narrow band of frequencies, a quarter of an octave wide, centered at 1000 Hz.

With a tool like this, you can create sonic pieces that fit together like a glove. Parametric equalizers are a great addition to any home studio. They are readily available in outboard configurations and some of the more expensive consoles even have built-in parametric equalization.

Video Example 4-5

Demonstration of Parametric Q and Sweep

Graphic EQ

This is called a graphic equalizer because it's the most visually graphic of all EQs. It's obvious, at a glance, which frequencies you've boosted or cut.

A graphic equalizer isn't appropriate to include in the channels of a mixer, simply because of the space required to contain 10 or more sliders, but it is a standard type of outboard EQ. The graphic EQs that we use in recording have 10, 31, or sometimes 15 individual sliders that each cut or boost a set frequency with a set bandwidth. The bandwidth on a 10-band graphic is one octave. The bandwidth on a 31-band graphic is one third of an octave.

Graphic equalizers were very popular in the studio a number of years ago. Today, graphic equalizers are used mostly in live sound reinforcement applications because they are convenient and very visual, and they work well in conjunction with acoustical measurement devices.

Notch Filter

A notch filter is used to seek and destroy problem frequencies, like a high-end squeal, ground hum or possibly a noise from a heater, fan, or camera.

Notch filters have a very narrow bandwidth and are often sweepable. These filters generally cut only.

Peaking Filters

All the equalizers we've covered, so far, are peaking filters because they cut or boost a band in a bell curved shape to a peak that is centered on the defining frequency. These are, by far, the most common types of equalizers.

Highpass Filter

A highpass filter lets the high frequencies pass through unaffected but cuts the low frequencies. In previous study of equalizers, we used in image of a bell curve with a center point at the selected frequency moving up or down as the frequency range was boosted or cut. Bandpass, highpass, and lowpass filters don't fit that picture. With these filters, we specify a frequency at which the cut begins. The selected frequency is called the *cutoff frequency*, or sometimes the *knee*. Once the filter point is defined, the severity of the cut (the steepness of the filter) is calibrated in dB per octave. This rate of the cut is called the *slope*. In their normal use, these filters cut at a rate between 6 and 12 dB per octave.

A highpass filter can help minimize 60-cycle hum on a particular track by filtering, or turning down, the fundamental frequency of the hum. Highpass filters function very well when you need to eliminate an ambient rumble, like a furnace in the background or street noise that leaks into a vocal mic.

Most modern highpass filters provide a sweepable frequency selector. In the context of creating a mix, a high pass filter is traditionally used to trim away unused or unnecessary low-frequency information. Simply listen to the track and sweep the highpass filter upward from the low-frequency range until you hear the low end thin out a little. Using filters in this manner is a good way to clean out unnecessary sonic ingredients. However, always be careful to critically assess the sonic impact on the overall mix. This is music, after all, and sometimes ingredients we don't consciously hear are indeed affecting the emotional or physical impact of the overall sound.

Types of Filters

Equalization comes in many forms. The first types of equalizers we covered were peaking filters, where a range of frequencies are cut or boosted in the form of a bell curve. In addition there are several forms of band adjusting filters, where an entire range of frequencies are adjusted uniformly. The icons typically used to indicate these filters accurately depict their functions.

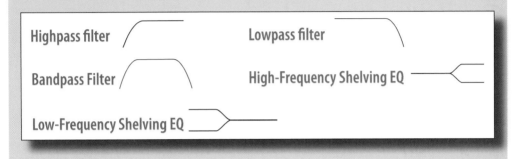

Lowpass Filter

A lowpass filter lets the low frequencies pass through unaffected and cuts the highs, usually above about 8 to 10 kHz. Lowpass filters have many uses. For instance, they can help minimize cymbal leakage onto the tom tracks, filter out a high buzz in a guitar amp, minimize tape hiss, or filter out string noise on a bass guitar track.

Listen to a track with the lowpass filter set with cutoff frequency as high as possible, then lower the cutoff frequency until you can hear the highs diminish. Then, raise the cutoff frequency slightly for a natural sound, while filtering out extraneous high frequencies. As with the highpass filter, always be careful to critically assess the sonic impact on the overall mix. You might be filtering frequencies that, even though you don't think you can hear them, are combining in the mix to create a sound or a feeling.

These filters, whether high-, low-, or bandpass, should be used to filter specific unwanted mix ingredients; they shouldn't be used to trim away at every track on the mix, just in case there's a problem in a frequency range.

Bandpass Filter

A bandpass filter lets us select a frequency range (a band) and let it pass through unaffected. In other words, all frequencies above and below a specified frequency range are filtered out. The bandpass filter is just like the marriage of a highpass and lowpass filter. With a bandpass filter, it's easy to create a lo-fi sound like that projected from a small transistor radio, or to zero in on any specific frequency range for a special effect.

Shelving EQ

A shelving EQ leaves all frequencies flat to a certain point, then turns all frequencies above or below that point down or up at a rate specified in dB per octave. As with high- and lowpass filters, shelving equalizers roll off the highs or lows, at a slope between 6 and 12 dB per octave; however, past the slope, all frequencies remain boosted or cut to the end of the frequency spectrum.

Shelving equalizers are a convenient way to add *air* (the high frequencies we can't necessarily hear as much as feel) to a mix. Simply sweep the cutoff frequency into the highs, above 12 kHz, or so, and raise the shelf slightly. This is a common technique, especially with the advent of the ultra-quiet gear available today. In a previous era, these high frequencies spelled a slow death by tape noise.

Combined Equalizers

Software-based equalizers emulate each type of hardware EQ. Many contain identical controls and even emulate the look and feel of highly respected classic equipment. Additionally, several software-based equalizers offer all the features we've discussed, all in one equalizer. In fact, most offer multiple options at each band.

The Equalizer's Sound

Equalizing circuitry does affect the sound of the source. In fact, there are equalizer that sound good, and equalizers that don't sound so good.

The quality, manufacturer, and design of any audio tool matters. Always listen to your music with and without the equalizer; be very discerning. It's better to avoid EQ rather than to use an EQ with lots of flexibility and a crummy sound.

Well-respected outboard gear gets that way because it works well and sounds good. Value reputation, yet always assess for yourself. Very inexpensive equalizers usually sound bad and are noisy—but not always. Very expensive equalizers usually sound great and are very clean and noise-free—but not always. It's up to you to listen and select the equipment that works for you.

Remember, even with the multitude of available equalizers, don't use EQ first to shape your sounds. First, get as close to the sound you want using mic choice and mic technique, then use EQ if it's necessary.

The Monitor Section

Some mixers have what is called the monitor section, which lets you listen to either the main outputs of the mixer or the tape tracks as they're coming back to the mixer from the multitrack. The switch that selects where each control hears from usually has two positions, bus and tape, or sometimes, input and tape.

This monitor section is used only for monitoring volumes and is totally separate from the recording level controls to the multitrack. Therefore, you can set exact levels to tape with the input faders, then turn their listening volume up or down in the monitor section.

Control Room Monitor Selector

The monitor selector is a very useful control center. It lets you listen to different buses or tape recorders in your setup simply by pressing the appropriate button on the board. This feature is usually located to the right of the channel faders.

If your mixdown recorder is normally connected to your mixer at a tape in point, if you have a CD player in your setup and if you have one or more aux buses available, the monitor selector is a particularly valuable tool.

The monitor selector on most mixers lets you listen to different buses without affecting what's going on in the other buses, including the signal path to the multitrack. While recording a band's basic tracks, you can eavesdrop on the headphone bus, just to get an idea of what their mix sounds like, or you can listen to an effects bus to verify which instruments are being sent to a reverb or delay.

Each manufacturer designs what they feel is the best array of features at the price point that makes sense for them. Even the most modest mixer offers some of these monitoring options. However, professional consoles are designed to be fast and efficient, so most of these monitoring functions are include.

Stereo to Mono

The Stereo/Mono switch does just what it says. It lets you listen to your song in whatever stereo image you've created with the pan controls, or it can take your stereo mix and combine it all into one mono mix (meaning that exactly the same thing comes from both the left and right speakers).

This is very useful, especially if you expect that your song will be played on a mono system at any time. Mono is standard for AM radio, television, and live sound reinforcement. If you'll be playing your band's demo tape as break music at a performance, be absolutely sure that the demo sounds great even in mono. Audio Example 4-44 demonstrates a simple stereo mix.

Audio Example 4-44

Simple Stereo Mix

Audio Example 4-45 uses the same mix, this time in mono.

Audio Example 4-45

Stereo Mix in Mono

Notice the change in sound between Audio Examples 4-44 and 4-45. With some changes in panning and delay times, this mix can work well in stereo and mono.

Stereo Master

The stereo master control is the final level adjustment out of the mixer going to the mixdown recorder or power amp. The level adjustment to the mixdown recorder is very important. A good mix for a commercial-sounding song, in most styles, should be fairly constant in its level.

Adjust the stereo master fader for the optimum reading on the stereo output meter. This level should be set specifically for the mixdown recorder. The stereo master fader is not for volume adjustment—it is for final output level adjustment. Use the monitor level control for listening volume.

Monitor Level/Speaker Level

Use the monitor level control to set listening levels. In a recording setting, unlike live sound reinforcement, there's a difference between listening level and level to the multitrack or mixdown recorder. Set levels using the channel faders and the stereo master L/R fader. Adjust listening levels using the monitor level/speaker level control.

Talkback/Communications

The talkback button lets you talk to someone listening to the headphone bus. Communication with musicians through the headphones is essential to efficient recording. A small microphone is often mounted on the mixer for this purpose. Some mixers have a separate mic input for a handheld or stand-mounted talkback mic.

Typically, talkback can also be routed onto the multitrack or mixdown recorders to add a verbal reference like the song title, date or artist. This verbal reference is called a *slate*. On vintage consoles, if a button has the word slate on it there's typically a low frequency (around 40 Hz) that's sent to the recorder with your voice. In fast rewind or fast forward during the shuttle of analog tape, this low frequency tone is heard as a beep, because the playback head picks up the magnetization as the tape speeds past the slate points. The slate beep is used to locate different songs on a reel.

Modern equipment really doesn't have much use for a slate tone, and most digital recording software offers excellent cataloging and locating features that we don't necessarily need to print titles, and the like, to the multitrack mixdown recorder. There are, however, times when this ability is convenient and efficient, especially in the commercial studio. Hence, large format recording consoles provide the flexibility to route the talkback to multiple destinations.

Test Tones

Your mixer might have a section marked tones, test tones, osc or oscillator, especially if you own a large format or vintage recording console. This section contains a frequency generator that produces different specific frequencies in their purest form—a sine wave. These frequencies are used to adjust input and output levels of your mixer, recorders and outboard equipment. Tones are used for electronic calibration and level setting, whereas pink and white noise are used for acoustical adjustments

Consider the stereo master output from your mixer to the mixdown recorder. Raise the level of the reference tone (between 500 and 1000 Hz) until the VU meter reads 0 VU on the stereo output of the mixer. Do this with the stereo master output faders set at the point where your mix level is correct. Adjust the tones level to the meters with the tones output control.

Fine-tune the left/right output balance. If one side reads slightly higher than the other, from the same 1 kHz tone, balance the two sides. Many mixers have separate level controls for left and right stereo outs. Proper adjustment of the left/right balance ensures the best accuracy in panning and stereo imaging.

Modern digital consoles and digital recorders are very stable in their levels and typically hassle free as far as level setting machine-to-machine recording levels.

Integrating Analog and Digital Recorders

Analog Reference Tones

One thousand Hz is the most common reference tone. A reference tone is an accurate representation of the average recording level. Therefore, if your mix level is correct and peaks at 0 VU or +1 or so, then this 1 kHz tone at 0 VU is an accurate gauge for setting levels for duplication of this particular song.

Patch the output of the mixer to the mixdown recorder and adjust the input level of the mixdown recorder to read 0 VU while the mixer

Patchbays

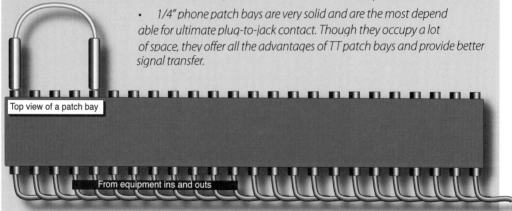

If all available ins and outs of your equipment are patched into the back of a patch bay, and if the corresponding points in the front of the patch bay are clearly labeled, your sessions will be more efficient. You'll free yourself from searching behind equipment in all sorts of contorted positions, just to connect two pieces of gear together. All patching can be done with short, easy-to-patch cables on the front of the patch bay. Patch bays are made using most standard types of jacks:

- RCA patch bays are the least expensive and work well when connecting gear with RCA connections. However, these do not allow for balanced ins and outs.

- TT (tiny telephone) patch bays use a small tip-ring-sleeve connector. These take the least amount of space and work very well in a professional studio where ins and outs must be balanced and massive amounts of patch points demand efficient use of space.

- 1/4" phone patch bays are very solid and are the most dependable for ultimate plug-to-jack contact. Though they occupy a lot of space, they offer all the advantages of TT patch bays and provide better signal transfer.

Top view of a patch bay

From equipment ins and outs

is showing 0 VU from the 1 kHz tone. We can now be sure that the level on the board matches the level on the mixdown machine.

Once these levels match, go ahead and record some of the 0 VU to your mixdown recorder so that when you make copies, you can use this as a reference tone to set the input levels of the duplicating machine.

If you're printing your entire mix to analog tape, there are certain procedures you should follow:

• Be sure your mixdown recorder is aligned and calibrated to work optimally with the specific brand and formulation of tape you're using. Refer to your owner's manuals for specifics to perform this setup or, better yet, hire a professional tech to get the analog recorder setup and matched to your mixer levels.

• Patch the mixdown master output from your mixer to the line inputs of your mixdown recorder.

• Set mixdown machine to record ready and, if available, select monitoring of the input or source.

• Set 0 VU as I specified above so that the mixer output and the mixdown recorder input read 0 VU.

• If your mixer has a tone generator or frequency oscillator, turn it on, select a frequency between 500 Hz and 1000 Hz, and raise the level on the mixdown master VUs on the mixer until they read 0 VU.

• At the beginning of the first reel of mixes, record the 0 VU tone. This is called a *reference tone*. If your master will be duplicated by a professional duplication facility, these tones let them adjust the level of their equipment to match yours. Following this procedure should result in a better, cleaner, and more accurate copy.

Next, record a series of tones that represent high, mid, and low frequencies. The standard frequencies to record at the beginning of a master tape are 100 Hz, 1 kHz, and 10 kHz. Giving the duplicator these references helps them compensate for any inherent problems in your equipment.

Patch Bays

A patchbay is nothing more than a panel with jacks in the front and jacks on the back. Jack #1 on the front is connected to Jack #1 on the back, #2 on the front to #2 on the back, and so on.

If all available ins and outs for all of your equipment are patched into the back of a patch bay and the corresponding points in the front of the patch bay are clearly labeled, you'll never need to search laboriously behind equipment again just to connect two pieces of gear together. All patching can be done with short, easy-to-patch cables on the front of the patch bay.

Patch bays are used for line level patches like channel ins and outs, tape recorder line ins and outs, sound module outputs and any signal processor ins and outs. Don't use the patch bay for powered outputs, like the speaker outputs of your power amplifiers.

The concept of easy and efficient patching becomes obvious when it's explained, and once you've made the move to include a patch bay in your setup, you'll be able to accomplish more, faster and more efficiently.

Most commercial recording facilities utilize patch bays extensively, simply because they are fast and efficient. When there are a few different types of projects moving through a studio each day, there's great value in quick and easy setups—this is the strength of the patch bay.

There is, however, a disadvantage to incorporating a patch bay into your system at home—it can degrade the sound quality. Patch bays are likely to rob something from the sound you're recording, especially if they're not impeccably cleaned and maintained or a regular basis. Anytime you plug a cable into almost anything, you risk some signal degradation.

Even when I'm tracking or mixing in a world-class recording facility, I eliminate any patch points that aren't absolutely necessary. I don't mind running a cable from one room to another, or under a door, or down the hall, because I've heard the difference in sound quality when I bypass unnecessary patches.

At home, you need to decide whether incorporating a patch bay is appropriate. If it makes your setup more efficient, in a way that enhances the creative freedom of your recording environment, that's the bottom line. I'm all for great sound, but what we do is all about great music.

Session Setup

Use this procedure as a starting point for your sessions. Start each session with your studio clean and all equipment adjusted to a predetermined typical level. Starting clean prevents problems resulting from unknown buttons being pushed in unknown places on the mixer.

Basic Procedure

- Move all channel faders to 0.
- Set input gain (preamp) and attenuator to lowest level.
- If you have only a mic/line switch, set it to line.
- Pan all channels to center.
- Set all EQ to flat (no boost or cut). If there is an EQ in/out switch, set it to out.
- Turn any auxiliary sends, effects sends or reverb sends all the way down or off.
- Set VU meters to allow monitoring of the final stereo output to the mixdown machine. If available, set other VU meters to monitor levels of aux buses to effects.
- Make sure there are no track assignments selected.
- Be sure there are no solo buttons selected.
- Be sure there are no mutes selected.

New Mixer Functions

Digital Audio Workstations, audio recording software, firewire interfaces, and control surfaces have radically changed the way we record audio. Though we'll study new technology in this series, the fundamental concepts in this chapter provide the necessary knowledge and insight that you'll need to build a powerful understanding of audio recording.

Being well versed in the recording world is the only way you'll be able to communicate with other enlightened musicians and engineers, and that constant communication can inspire your individual growth and possibly open doors into the business world of music and recording.

The mixer can be your most flexible means of achieving the musical sounds that you want. Go to your own setup and find what kind of controls you have. Review this material thoroughly and apply each point, deliberately, to your own setup.

A thorough understanding of the information in this chapter is necessary as a foundation for upcoming chapters. We'll build on this foundation in a methodical, easy-to-follow way. Each chapter is structured, using combined media, to closely resemble a private lesson.

If you do the assignments and study the DVD, text, and illustrations, you'll see a marked difference in your recording skills and end results.

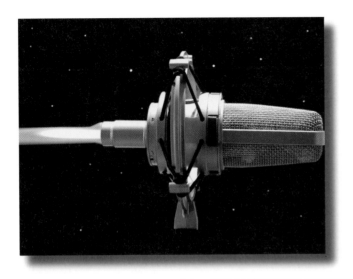

5

Microphones: Our Primary Tools

There's much more to mic choice than finding a trusted manufacturer that you can stick with. There's much more to mic placement than simply setting the mic close to the sound source. The difference between mediocre audio recordings and exemplary audio recordings is quite often defined by the choice and placement of microphones.

The microphone is our most fundamental tool. You can have $100,000 worth of esoteric, vintage, high-tech gear in the your signal path, but if the microphone doesn't capture the sonic essence that's perfect for the recording, it's all a waste. Each microphone offers a sonic personality and offers the potential to be much more than just an archival tool. For instance, if you and a buddy test 10 mics on Joe to see how they'll work for his new song, nine of the microphones might evoke agreement that, yeah, that sounds like Joe. However, chances are that one of the 10 mics might get the response, "Wow! Joe sounds great on this mic!"

Once you find the microphone that sounds great for whatever sound source you're recording, it's time to compare other options in the signal path, such as preamplifiers, compressors, or equalizers—the fewer additions to the signal path, between the mic and the recorder, the better. Musically, you need to do what you need to do. As long as it feeds the passion and emotion of the music, it's alright to include a hundred processors in the signal path; however, if you want to capture the true essence of the original sound at the source, find the perfect mic and the perfect preamp, patch directly into the recorder, and record.

If you need to use compression, make it a conscious choice, and be sure the compressor is enhancing the musical impact. In the modern era, noise isn't really an issue, so you can always add compression and other processing during mixdown. Save as many musical decisions as possible for mixdown.

Audio Example 5-1

Six Different Types of Microphones on the Same Source

Video Example 5-1

Five Different Types of Microphones on the Same Source

As we cover techniques for recording different instruments, we'll consistently need to consider microphone choice and technique. The MIDI era led us away from the art of acoustic recording but as time has proceeded, acoustic recordings of drums, guitars, strings, brass, percussion and sound effects have returned. There is a kind of life to an acoustic recording that can only truly exist through recording real instruments played by real people in an acoustical environment.

We can increase the life in our MIDI sounds by running them into an amplification system, then miking that sound. We might or might not need to include the direct sound of the MIDI sound module.

Using a mic to capture sound is not as simple as just selecting the best mic. There are two other critically important factors involved in capturing sound:

+ Where we place the mic in relation to the sound source
+ The acoustical environment in which we choose to record the sound source

As you'll see in the audio examples in this course, the sound of the acoustical environment plays a very important role in the overall sound quality.

Selecting a microphone involves more than a simple random search for "the sound." Our understanding of mics and how they work, along with the ability to read and understand their specifications, will allows to make educated predictions regarding which mics to consider. You should be able to listen to a source, and then make an intelligent decision about which mics to audition.

Technically, we must consider a set of factors when choosing a microphone: directional characteristic, operating principle, response characteristic, and output characteristic. In addition, the real-world considerations are always cost, durability, and appearance. In today's market, there are several very inexpensive mics available that look great. Some of them sound okay, but if you need some impressive looking mics, for your clients' sake, consider them like a decoration. However, if you intend to make great music and are serious about your craft, always be in search of great-sounding microphones.

Directional Characteristic

Pickup Pattern/Polar Pattern

Any time you mic a source, you must be aware of which way to aim the mic, and whether that particular mic is sensitive only to the intended source. Understanding the microphone *polar response pattern*, also called the *pickup pattern*, is fundamental to capturing the essence of the sound you intentionally want. There are three basic polar patterns we consider when comparing and choosing microphones: omnidirectional, bidirectional, and unidirectional.

We typically refer to the overall pickup in our discussions; however, each polar response will vary dramatically when frequency ranges are compared. In addition, there are variations of the directional characteristics. Because of the way most directional characteristics are created, high frequencies are the most directional and low frequencies are least directional.

Polar Patterns

Polar graphs are seen in two dimensions, but they imply three dimensions. All patterns should be visualized in a spherical three dimensional plane.

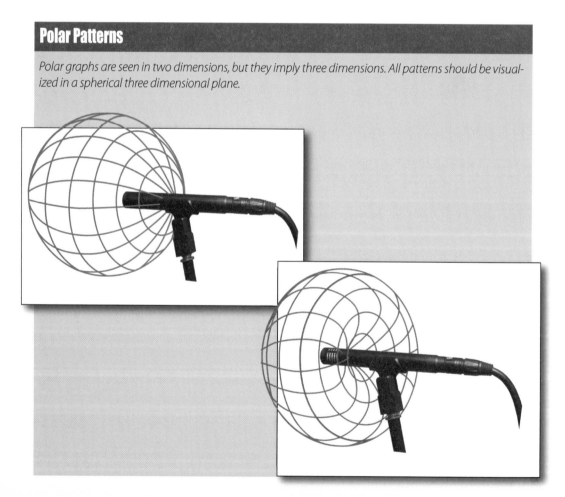

The polar response pattern is not usually a result of the inherent operational principle of the microphone capsule. More often, it is the result of the physical housing, or a combination, and electronic balance of multiple diaphragms.

Polar Response Graph

The polar response graph provides a visual image of the microphone's sensitivity to sound coming from different directions. This circular graph indicates sensitivity in a 360-degree circular scope and is interpreted as a three-dimensional image, even though it's drawn two-dimensional for the sake of simplicity.

On-Axis

Zero degrees, on the graph, represents the front of the microphone (the portion designed to pick up the sound). This position is referred to as *on-axis*.

Off-Axis

Any position on the polar response graph that isn't on-axis is called *off-axis* and is quantified in degrees. 180 degrees, on the graph, represents the back of the mic (the part directly in back of the portion designed to pick up the sound); it's referred to as 180 degrees off-axis.

A microphone, which demonstrates a decrease in sensitivity at a certain point on the polar graph is said to discriminate from sound at that point. We indicate that decrease in sensitivity by denoting its degree marker. A microphone with reduced sensitivity at 180 degrees on the graph is said to exhibit 180-degree *off-axis discrimination*.

Additionally, for the sake of indicating discrimination the graph is considered symmetrical. Indicating that a microphone exhibits 150 degree off-axis discrimination indicates that the point of least sensitivity is at 150 degrees, and since the graph is symmetric also at 210 degrees.

Polar Response Graph

The polar response graph plots the spacial sensitivity as it relates to the position of the sound source in relation to the microphone capsule. These graphs are considered symmetrical in relation to the plotted sensitivity and, in addition, should be considered three-dimensionally spherical.

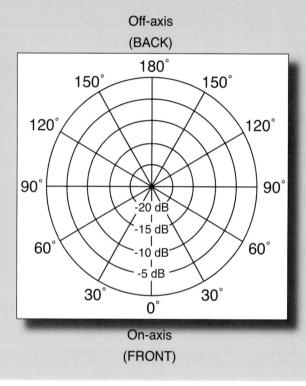

This also indicates that there is sensitivity, to some degree, in the region centered on 180-degrees off-axis.

Each microphone uses a design that exhibits a unique polar response throughout the frequency spectrum.

Because of the symmetrical aspect of the polar graph, sometimes they're indicated, 0 – 180 degrees left and right instead of 360 degrees around. This is actually a little simpler system, since off-axis discrimination is always referenced as 180 degrees or less, with the symmetry across the 0 degree axis implied.

Polar Shapes

The two most basic polar response patterns are omnidirectional (doesn't discriminate against sounds from any direction) and cardioid (discriminates against sound that are 180 degrees off-axis). The other two polar shapes in this illustration are bidirectional (an omnidirectional pattern on each side off the mic) and hypercardioid (a bidirectional pattern with a large half and a small half).

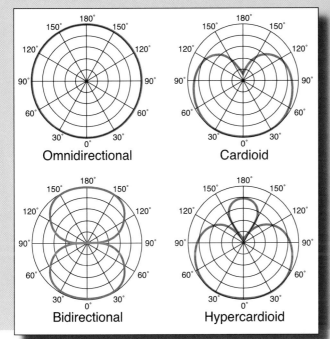

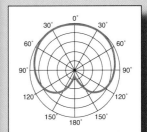

Sometimes the on-axis position is noted at the top of the graph; other times it's noted at the bottom. In either case, the 0° position is always the front of the mic.

Sensitivity Scale

The polar response graph calibrates spherical sensitivity through a series of concentric circles. Each concentric circle is consecutively smaller. The outer circle indicates full sensitivity (0 dB decrease insensitivity) and there are typically four or five consecutively smaller circles between the outer circle and the center point, each typically indicating a decrease in sensitivity of 5 dB. Plotting the decreases of sensitivity around the polar graph is what creates the polar pattern.

Some polar graphs include an additional outer circle, at +5 dB, for the rare instance that certain frequencies sum, creating a hypersensitivity, which exceeds the normal full sensitivity.

Multiple Frequencies and Symmetry on the Polar Graph

The polar graph often displays the directional characteristic for multiple frequencies. To accomplish this in the least cluttered manner, all patterns are assumed to be symmetrical across the Y axis. In addition, to help clarify the results, various line styles are incorporated on each frequency. Sometimes the polar graph is split, like the graph on the left, to highlight the variations in frequency response; other times the graph is whole, like the graph on the right, with the pattern variations simply changing between left and right.

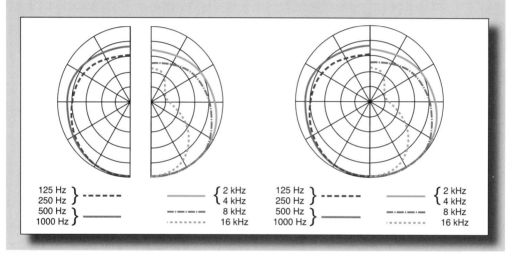

125 Hz ⎫	-------		2 kHz ⎫	125 Hz ⎫	-------		2 kHz ⎫
250 Hz ⎬			4 kHz ⎬	250 Hz ⎬			4 kHz ⎬
500 Hz ⎫	—·—·—	8 kHz	500 Hz ⎫	—·—·—	8 kHz
1000 Hz ⎭	········	16 kHz	1000 Hz ⎭	········	16 kHz

Normally, the pattern on the graph, which is visually dominant and uses a solid bold line, is the average overall pattern and is typically measured from a 1 kHz sine wave. Many electronic measurements consider a 1 kHz sine wave as the reference, or average, signal across the audible spectrum.

Omnidirectional

An omnidirectional mic, sometimes referred to simply as *omni*, hears equally from all directions. It doesn't reject sound from anywhere. An omnidirectional pickup pattern provides the fullest sound from a distance. Omni microphones are very good at capturing room ambience, recording groups of instruments that you can gather around one mic, and capturing a vocal performance while still letting the acoustics of the room interact with the sound of the voice.

Omnidirectional Pickup Pattern

Mics with an omnidirectional pickup pattern pick up sound equally from all directions and don't reject sound from any direction.

Omnidirectional microphones are inappropriate in a live setting because they produce feedback more quickly than any other pickup pattern.

Bidirectional

Bidirectional microphones hear equally from the sides, but they don't hear from the edges. Bidirectional microphones are an excellent choice for recording two sound sources to one track with the most intimacy and least adverse phase interaction and room sound. Position the mic between the sound sources for the best blend. Once you've committed the sound to one tape track, there's not much you can do to fix a bad balance or blend.

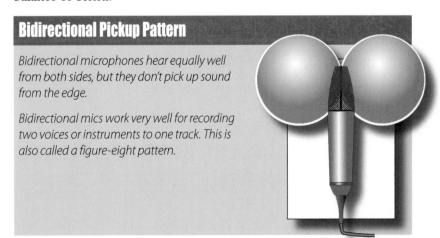

Bidirectional Pickup Pattern

Bidirectional microphones hear equally well from both sides, but they don't pick up sound from the edge.

Bidirectional mics work very well for recording two voices or instruments to one track. This is also called a figure-eight pattern.

Unidirectional

Most microphones demonstrate a unidirectional characteristic, often called a directional or cardioid pickup pattern. The pickup pattern is visually represented by a heart-shape—rounded in front and dimpled in the back. The unidirectional mic is most sensitive (hears the best) at the part of the mic into which you sing; it's least sensitive (hears the worst) at the side opposite the part into which you sing.

The advantage to using a microphone with a cardioid pickup pattern lies in the ability to isolate sounds. You can point the mic at one instrument while you're pointing it away from another instrument. The disadvantage to a cardioid pickup pattern is that it will typically only give you a full sound from a close proximity to the sound source. Once you're a foot or two away from the sound source, a cardioid pickup pattern produces a very thin-sounding rendition of the sound you're miking.

In a live sound setting, directional mics are almost always best because they produce far less feedback than mics with omnidirectional or bidirectional pickup patterns.

There are five directional pickup patterns for consideration in normal use: cardioid, supercardioid, hypercardioid, ultracardioid, and subcardioid. Here is a comparison of their fundamental polar response patterns. Each microphone is unique in design and may exhibit its own rendition of these response patterns. Also, keep in mind that, throughout the frequency spectrum, results may vary.

Cardioid

The cardioid pickup pattern demonstrates full response at the front of the microphone and a decrease in sensitivity of up to 25 or 30 dB at 180 degrees off-axis.

Cardioid Pickup Pattern

A microphone with a cardioid pickup pattern hears sound best from the front and actively rejects sounds from behind. With its heart-shaped pickup pattern, you can point the mic toward the sound you want to record and away from the sound you don't want to record.

In relation to a cardioid pickup pattern, the supercardioid, and hypercardioid pickup patterns each become progressively narrower on the sides, with an increased area of off-axis sensitivity.

Supercardioid

A microphone with a supercardioid polar response is more directional at the front, than a microphone exhibiting a cardioid pattern, with a decreased sensitivity on the sides and an area of sensitivity about 170 degrees off-axis.

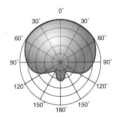

Hypercardioid

A microphone with a hypercardioid polar response exhibits a high degree of directionality at the front, with a decrease of about 12 dB on the sides and an area of least sensitivity at about 110 degrees off-axis.

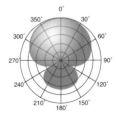

Ultracardioid

A microphone with an ultracardioid polar response is very focused and directional in front with a small area of sensitivity at 90 degrees and 180 degrees.

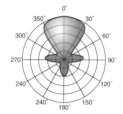

Subcardioid

The subcardioid polar response is wider and extends further than the cardioid pattern, approaching the non-directionality of an omnidirectional microphone.

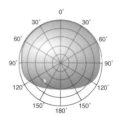

Operating Principle

Although there are hundreds of different microphones available from a lot of manufacturers, they essentially all fit into three basic categories: condenser, moving-coil, and ribbon. Condenser and moving-coil mics are the most common of these three, although they may all be used in recording, as well as live, situations.

There are other types of microphones with operating principles that differ from what we will cover in this course, and each type of microphone has its own individual personality. Mic types other than condenser, moving-coil, and ribbon are usually selected for a special effect in a situation where the music needs a unique sound that enhances the emotional impact of the song.

Transducer Types

A transducer is any device that transforms one type of energy into another type of energy. For instance, a speaker converts electrical energy into acoustic energy. The amplifier sends an electronic signal (a continuously varying flow of electrons) to the speaker, which responds to the electronic signal by moving air, which is, at that point, acoustical energy. Your ear is another example of a transducer because it converts the acoustic energy into electrical energy, which is then sent to the audio perception portion of your brain.

Whether in a recording or live sound application, the microphone is the first transducer, past the source, in our signal path. The microphone converts acoustic energy into electrical energy. There are other transducers that might have been involved prior to the actual sound source. For our purposes in audio, we'll consider the microphone as the first transducer within our control.

Of the three types of microphone we'll study there are only two types of transducers: *magnetic induction* and *variable capacitance*. The transducer is the actual microphone capsule—the point where the acoustic energy from the sound source reaches the mic and begins the flow of electrons. The microphone might contain amplifying circuitry, which is insignificant in our understanding of transducer functionality.

Magnetic Induction Transducers

A magnetic induction transducer utilizes and process where metal, which has magnetic properties (in other words, it can be magnetized), is stimulate into motion around, or is attached to, a magnet. Of the three mic types that we'll study, two use magnetic transducers: moving-coil and ribbon.

Mics that use magnetic induction, whether moving-coil or ribbon, are *dynamic microphones*. Often, moving-coil mics are generically referred to as dynamic microphones, and ribbon microphones are differentiated as … ribbon microphones. It is more accurate to differentiate them as moving-coil and ribbon mics.

Variable Capacitance Transducers

Variable capacitance transducers operate on an electrostatic, rather than a magnetic, principle. A variable capacitance microphone capsules utilizes a fixed, solid conductive plate adjacent to flexible piece of plastic that's been coated with a conductive alloy—often containing gold.

A capacitor is a device that stores an electrical charge. When the moveable plate is electrically charged an electrostatic charge is stored between the two surfaces. As sound waves vibrate the alloy-coated plastic diaphragm, the area of stored electrical charge emits a continuously varying flow of electrons that accurately portray the waveform. Variable capacitance transducers require power to charge the plates and to power an amplifying circuit within the microphone.

A microphone that use a variable capacitance transducer is sometimes called a capacitance microphone, although more often it's referred to as a condenser microphone. The old-school name for a capacitor was *condenser*—same device, different name.

Operating Principle of the Moving-Coil Mic

A moving-coil microphone operates on a magnetic principle. When an object that can be magnetized is moved around a magnet, there is a change in the energy within the magnet. There is also a continual variation in the magnetic status of the object moving in relation to the magnet. The moving-coil microphone uses this fact to transfer the changing air pressure, produced by an audio waveform, into a continually varying flow of electrons that can be received by the mic preamp.

In a moving-coil mic, a coil of thin copper wire is suspended over a fixed magnet, enabling the coil to move up and down around the magnet. A thin mylar plastic diaphragm closes the top of the coil and serves to receive the audio waves. As the crests and troughs of the continually varying audio waveform reach the diaphragm, the coil is forced to move around the magnet. The movement of the copper coil

Moving-Coil Microphones

Copper wire is wrapped into a cylinder. This cylinder is then suspended around a magnet. The copper coil moves up and down in response to pressure changes caused by sound waves.

The crest of the audio wave moves the coil down, causing a change in the coil magnetism. The trough of the audio wave moves the coil up, again causing a change in the coil magnetism.

As the coil moves around the magnet it receives a continually varying magnetic image. The continually varying magnetism will ideally mirror the changing air pressure from the sound wave. This continually varying magnetism is the origin of the signal that arrives at the mixer's mic input.

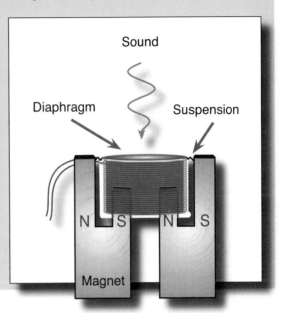

around the magnet is what causes the changing flow of electrons that represent the sound wave.

Operating Principle of the Ribbon Mic

A ribbon microphone operates on a magnetic principle like the moving-coil. A metallic ribbon is suspended between two poles of a magnet. As the sound wave vibrates the thin ribbon, the magnetic flow changes in response, causing a continually varying flow of electrons. As the ribbon moves between the poles of the magnet, it is being magnetized in varying degrees of north and south magnetism, in direct proportion to the changes in amplitude produced by the sound wave. This continually varying flow of electrons is the origin of the signal that reaches the microphone input of your mixer.

Historically, ribbon microphones have been very fragile; the ribbons needed to be a certain length to generate enough signal strength and

Ribbon Microphones

A thin metal ribbon suspended between two poles of a magnet vibrates in response to each crest and trough of a sound wave. As the ribbon moves in the magnetic field, it continually varies in its magnetism. These changes of magnetism are the origin of the signal that is sent to the mic input of your mixer.

The signal produced by the ribbon is typically weaker than the signal produced by the moving-coil. In practical terms, that means you'll usually need more preamplification at the mic input to achieve a satisfactory line level signal.

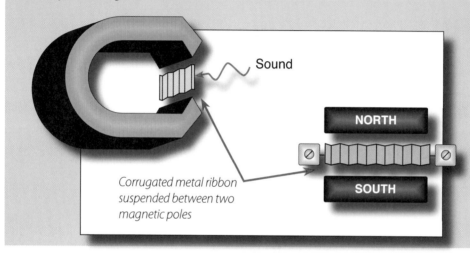

Sound

NORTH

SOUTH

Corrugated metal ribbon suspended between two magnetic poles

they needed to be thin enough to respond accurately to sonic nuance. Therefore, vintage ribbon mics like the RCA 77 DX, though they sound great, constantly need maintenance.

Modern ribbon microphones are capable of using smaller, stronger magnets, which enables the use of shorter ribbons. This has resulted in the production of more durable ribbon mics, although they still are the most fragile of the three types we use.

Since ribbon mics operate on a magnetic principle, they don't require a power source to operate, although there are some new ribbon mics that use phantom power to drive internal amplification circuitry—phantom power can be damaging to ribbon mics other than these. A vintage microphone ribbon tends to act like a fuse when it receives phantom power—it blows (pop, kaput, gone, send in for replacement … get my point?).

Operating Principle of the Condenser Mic

Condenser mics operate on a fairly simple premise, although it is physically based on a different principle. Whereas, the moving-coil and ribbon microphones operate on magnetic inductance principle, the condenser mic is based on a variable capacitance principle.

A charged (positive or negative) electrical current is applied to a metal-coated piece of plastic. The plastic is a little like the plastic wrap you keep on your leftover food. The metallic coating is thin enough to vibrate in response to sound waves; in fact, the technique used to apply the coating to the membrane is called *sputtering* because the alloy is so lightly applied. Its function is to provide conductivity for the electrical charge while not inhibiting the flexibility of the plastic membrane. The ingredients of the alloy vary from manufacturer to manufacturer, but the key factor is conductivity—it must be able to carry an electrical charge.

The metal-coated plastic will vibrate when it's subjected to an audio wave because of the physical reality called sympathetic vibration. The principle of sympathetic vibration says, if it is possible for a surface to vibrate at a specific frequency, it will vibrate when it is in the presence of a sound wave containing that frequency. The metal-coated plastic membrane, the *diaphragm,* in a condenser microphone must be able to sympathetically vibrate when in the presence of any audio wave in our audible frequency spectrum.

This metal-coated piece of plastic is positioned close to a solid piece of metallic alloy, called a backplate. As the moveable plate is electrically charged, or *polarized*, electrical energy begins to accumulate between the two metallic surfaces. The area of electrically charged air between the diaphragm and the backplate is called the dielectric.

Condenser Microphone Capsule

The membrane of the condenser mic is very thin and vibrates in response to sounds. It is lightly coated with a metallic alloy so that it can conduct electricity. The crest of a sound wave moves the metal-coated plastic membrane inward. The trough moves it outward. The moveable plate is continually responding to the varying air pressure caused by the sounds around it.

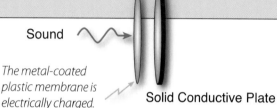

Sound

The metal-coated plastic membrane is electrically charged.

Solid Conductive Plate

As the moveable plate is charged, electricity stores between the solid and moveable conductive surfaces. This area of stored charge, called the dielectric, is really just electrically charged air. A system like this that stores an electrical charge is called a capacitor.

Dielectric

The moveable plate responds to the crest of a sound wave by moving inward, creating a discharge of the dielectric.

The trough of a sound wave pulls the moveable plate outward, varying the discharge of the dielectric.

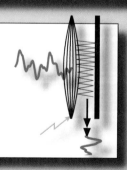

The continually changing pressure on the moveable plate causes a continual variation in the discharge of the dielectric. This continually varying discharge will (ideally) mirror the sound wave's changes in air pressure. Condenser mics excel at this process because of the low mass of the metal-coated membrane (the diaphragm) and the simplicity of displacing electrically charged air.

As the crest and trough of a sound wave meet the thinly coated plastic, the plastic vibrates sympathetically with the sound wave. As the diaphragm vibrates, the area, between the solid metal surface and the moveable metal surface, changes. These changes in the dielectric create a discharge of electrical current. This electrical discharge exactly represents the changing energy in the sound wave. In other words, you have an electrical version of the acoustic energy you started with at the sound source.

Since there is very little mass in the condenser microphone's metal-coated membrane, it responds very quickly and accurately when in the presence of sound. Therefore, the condenser capsule is very efficient at capturing sounds with high transient content as well as sounds with interesting complexities.

The signal that comes from the capsule is very weak and must be amplified to mic level. Most condenser mics use transistors in the internal amplifying circuitry; transistors provide a very clean and accurate amplification. Some condenser microphones utilize a vacuum tube instead of the transistor because of the smooth and warm sound they produce. Many of these tube microphones are well respected and highly acclaimed.

Once the signal from the mic reaches the mixer, it's boosted to line level at the input preamp.

Phantom Power

The capsule of a condenser microphone requires power to charge the metal-coated membrane. Power is also required to amplify the signal from the capsule up to microphone level.

Some condenser microphones will house a battery to power the capsule and the amplifying circuitry. However, *phantom power* provides a more efficient way to power to the condenser mic because it's efficient, constant, and reliable. The phantom power supply is typically in the mixer. The power is sent to the mic through the balanced mic cable.

If you use batteries to power a condenser mic, always be sure the batteries are fresh and that they're supplying sufficient voltage to optimally run the microphone's circuitry.

If your mixer doesn't provide phantom power, use a commercially manufactured external phantom power supply. It receives 120 volt AC current and transforms it to the proper DC voltage and amperage. External mic preamplifiers also supply phantom power.

Phantom power does not pose an electrical danger to the user since phantom power is low voltage and very low amperage DC current. Phantom power voltage is typically 48 volts although it can range from around 11 volts to 48 volts. Each condenser mic draws current from the phantom power supply based on its electrical needs.

Amperage is the force behind current measured in a unit called an amp. A milliamp is one thousandth of an amp. Condenser mics draw a very low-amperage DC current, ranging from less than 1 mA (less than one one-thousandth of an amp) to about 12 mA. By comparison a typical household circuit carries 15 to 50 amps of 120-volt AC current.

Phantom power has no adverse effect on the audio signal being carried by the mic cable. The DC voltage is applied equally to pins 2 and 3 of the XLR connection relative to pin 1, which is at ground potential. The fact that it functions undetected in the background on the same cable the mic signal travels on, explains the term "phantom" power.

Vintage tube mics often don't require phantom power from the mixer because the power supply is external to the mic. The external power supply receives 120-volt AC current, which provides power to the external amplifying circuitry; the charging voltage for the capsule element is provided by the external power supply. The mic connects to the power supply, and then the power supply connects to the mixer input.

Electret Condenser Microphones

An electret condenser microphone utilizes a permanently charged capsule, which doesn't require phantom power. However, power is still required to operate the internal preamp. Phantom power can still be used to power the microphone, but the decreased electrical requirements make this condenser mic efficient while receiving battery power. Consequently, electret condensers are an excellent choice for application in the field. They possess all the sonic benefits of the condenser design with a realistic expectation the battery power will provide sufficient longevity.

Comparison Between Moving-Coil, Ribbon, and Condenser Microphones

If you possess the basic understanding of each mic type, and if you have a grasp on how each type works, you'll be able to make very good microphone selections. The microphone you select for your specific recording situation makes a big difference to the sound of the final recording. It's almost pathetic how easy it is to get great sounds when you've selected the right mic for the job and you've run the mic through a high-quality preamp.

Whereas the diaphragm of the microphone is the vibrating membrane that responds to sound waves, its makeup plays a key role in the inherent ability of the microphone to provide an accurate version of the sound it receives. Since we know that the moving-coil capsule utilizes a membrane attached to the top of a coil of copper wire, and since the sound wave must move the entire assembly around a magnet, we can draw the simple deduction that, by nature of its mass, it is physically less responsive than either the ribbon or condenser capsule. In fact, this deduction is true. Condenser mics are the most accurate and responsive of the three mic types, and ribbon mics are typically more accurate than moving-coil mics. Though there may be anomalies to this comparison, it is generally accepted.

Moving-Coil Mics

Though moving-coil mics don't excel in capturing transients and subtleties, you can still take advantage of their tendencies and characteristics.

Moving-coil mics are the standard choice for most live situations, but they are also very useful in the studio. Here are some examples of popular and trustworthy moving-coil microphones:

+   Shure SM57, SM58, SM7
+   Electro-Voice RE20
+   Sennheiser 421, 441
+   Audio-Technica ATM25, Pro-25
+   AKG D12, D112, D3500, D1000E
+   Beyer M88

Moving-coil mics are the most durable of all the mic types. They also withstand the most volume before they distort within their own circuitry.

A moving-coil mic typically colors a sound more than a condenser mic. This coloration usually falls in the frequency range between about 5 kHz and 10 kHz. As long as we realize that this coloration is present, we can use it to our advantage. In our studies on EQ, we've found that this frequency range can add clarity, presence, and understandability to many vocal and instrumental sounds.

Moving-coil mics have a thin sound when they are more than about a foot from the sound source. They're usually used in close-mic applications, with the mic placed anywhere from less than an inch from the sound source up to about 12 inches from the sound source.

Since moving-coil mics can withstand a lot of volume, they sound the best in close-mic applications; and since they add high-frequency edge, they're good choices for miking electric guitar speaker cabinets, bass drum, snare drum, toms, or any loud instrument that benefits from close-mic technique. Use them when you want to capture lots of sound with lots of edge from a close distance and aren't as concerned about subtle nuance and literal accuracy of the original waveform.

Moving-coils are also used in live performances for vocals. They work well in close-miking situations, add high-frequency clarity, and are very durable.

Condenser Microphones

Condenser microphones are the most accurate. They respond to fast attacks and transients more precisely than other types, and they typically add the least amount of tonal coloration. The large vocal mics used in professional recording studios are usually examples of condenser mics. Condenser mics also come in much smaller sizes and interesting shapes. Some popular condenser mics are

- Shure KSM 44, KSM 32, KSM 27, KSM 141, KSM 137, KSM 109 , SM 82
- Neumann U87, U89, U47, U67, TLM170, KM83, KM84, KM184, TLM193
- AKG 414, 451, 391, 535, C1000, 460, C3000, C-12, The Tube
- Electro-Voice BK-1
- Sennheiser MKH 40, MKH 80

- B&K 4011
- Blue Microphones Bluebird, Bottle, Cactus, Kiwi, Mouse, Dragon Fly, Blueberry, Baby Bottle
- Audio-Technica 4033, 4050, 4047, 4060, 4041
- Milab DC96B
- Schoeps CMC 5U
- Groove Tube MD-2, MD-3
- Crown PZM-30D

Use a condenser microphone whenever you want to accurately capture the true sound of a voice or instrument. Condensers are almost always preferred when recording

- Acoustic guitar
- Acoustic piano
- Vocals
- Real brass
- Real strings
- Woodwinds
- Percussion
- Acoustic room ambience

Condenser microphones (especially in omni configuration) typically capture a broader range of frequencies from a greater distance than the other mic types. In other words, you don't need to be as close to the sound source to get a full sound. This trait of condenser microphones is a great advantage in the recording studio because it enables us to record a full sound while still including some of the natural ambience in a room. The further the mic is from the sound source, the more influential the ambience is on the recorded sound.

Condenser microphones that work wonderfully in the studio often provide poor results in a live sound reinforcement situation. Since they have a flat frequency response, these condenser mics tend to feed back more quickly than microphones designed specifically for live sound applications (especially in the low-frequency range). There are many condenser mics designed for sound reinforcement, and there are many condenser mics that work very well in either setting. Condenser mics often have a low-frequency roll-off switch that lets you decrease low-frequency sensitivity. In a live audio situation, the low-frequency roll-off is effective in reducing low-frequency feedback.

Ribbon Mics

Ribbon mics are the most fragile of all the mic types. This one factor makes them less useful in a live sound reinforcement application, even though ribbon mics produced within the last 10 or 15 years are much more durable than the older classic ribbon mics.

The ribbon capsule is inherently bidirectional. Both the front and back of the ribbon are equally sensitive and sound from the 90 degrees off-axis cancels. Many manufacturers take advantage of this natural characteristic and produce bidirectional ribbon mics. On the other hand, there are several ribbon mics that exhibit a unidirectional characteristic; these mics utilize a ribbon with the back (180 degrees off-axis) enclosed. Once the back of the ribbon is enclosed the capsule is inherently omnidirectional, like the moving-coil and condenser capsules.

Ribbon mics, exhibiting a unidirectional polar characteristic, are like moving-coil mics in that they color the sound source by adding a high-frequency edge, and they generally have a thin sound when used in a distant miking setup. When used as a close mic, ribbon microphones can have a full sound that is often described as being warmer and smoother than a moving-coil.

There are some great-sounding ribbon microphones available. Some of the commonly used ribbon microphones are

- Beyer M160, M500
- RCA 77-DX, 44 BY, 10001
- AEA R84, R44C, R88
- Royer SF-12. SF 24

Ribbon mics are fragile and need to be used in situations where they won't be dropped or jostled. If you use a ribbon mic to record drums and the drummer hits the mic too many times with his stick, the ribbon will break. Repairs like this can be costly. After breaking a couple of these mics, I decided it might be best if I stuck to one of the tried and true, very durable choices. I still tend to use the Beyer M160 ribbon a lot when I'm recording drum samples because I like the sound, but sampling is a very controlled mic usage, and I'm usually the only one around with a drum stick.

The Shaping of the Pickup Pattern

Inherent Pickup Patterns

The inherent polar response characteristic of the moving-coil and basic condenser capsules is omnidirectional. Set in space with no physical housing, they are equally sensitive to sound from all directions—they don't reject sound from any direction. The inherent polar response characteristic of the ribbon capsule is bidirectional. Set in space, with no physical housing, it is equally sensitive to sound from the front and back but it is not sensitive to sounds coming from the sides—it rejects sounds 90 and 270 degrees off-axis.

Whereas the moving-coil and condenser capsule are inherently omnidirectional, and the ribbon capsule is inherently bidirectional, in design and application the majority of microphones ever manufactured exhibit a cardioid polar response. Polar response characteristics are designed and create in two fundamental ways: physical housing design and electrical combinations of multiple capsules.

Physical Housing Design

Most microphone designs use the physical housing around the capsule to shape directional characteristics. The concept is simple once you understand phase interactions between sound waves—amplitudes in-phase sum, and amplitudes out of phase cancel. For physical shaping of

Creating the Cardioid Pickup Pattern

A microphone with selectable pickup patterns, typically uses a variance in relative polarizing voltage between the front and back sides of the condenser capsule to shape the pattern between omnidirectional, bidirectional, and variations of the cardioid patterns. Other mic designs utilize the physical design of the mic housing to influence the polar pattern.

The ports on the sides of the housing provide an alternate pathway to the mic capsule for off-axis sounds. As sounds travel around the mic, though the ports, and arrive at the front and back of the diaphragm, they reduce in level because of phase cancellation. The position and quantity of the ports determines the specific frequencies that are rejected most.

The microphone below is a Shure KSM141. It switches from cardioid to omnidirectional characteristic by sliding an internal cylinder up to cover the ports.

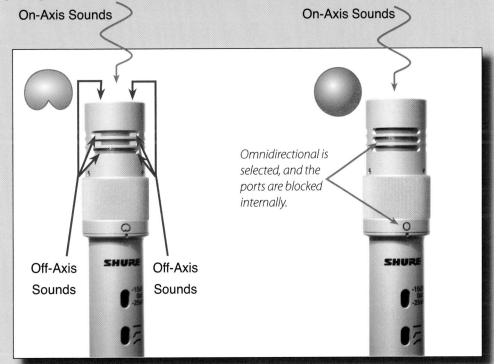

On-Axis Sounds

On-Axis Sounds

Omnidirectional is selected, and the ports are blocked internally.

Off-Axis
Sounds

Off-Axis
Sounds

directional characteristic, the ribbon capsule is omnidirectional because the back of the ribbon is enclosed.

Microphones that contain a capsule at the top of a barrel housing with slots (we could also say openings, or ports) around the capsule end, exhibit a unidirectional polar response. It is these ports that shape the directional characteristic. On-axis sound waves stimulate the diaphragm in the normal way; however, off-axis sound waves are allowed to reach the front and/or back of the diaphragm via multiple routes, provided by the ports around the housing. As the off-axis waveforms combine at the diaphragm, the fact that they've arrived at the same point (the diaphragm) through various pathways (around the mic, and through the network of ports) indicates that the length of their journey varies with the pathway. Since the same off-axis waveform has been split, and since each pathway is a different distance from the origination of the waveform, phase interaction is built into the design. The key in the mic design is the positioning and quantity of the ports. The intent of the designer is to allow negative phase interaction of off-axis waveforms, through the series of ports in the physical housing, as they travel multiple off-axis pathways.

If the ports are covered up, these microphones become omnidirectional rather than cardioid. If fact, some manufacturers offer multiple capsules for use with the same microphone body. The capsules typically screw on and off and their only physical difference is that the cardioid capsule has ports and the omni capsule doesn't.

Audio Example 5-2

Acoustic Guitar Miked Using Multiple Polar Patterns

The large format condenser microphone controls directional characteristic electrically rather than through the design of the physical housing. These microphones are designed for and used in the studio and are rarely seen in a live setting; they're large, expensive, fragile, and adversely affected by environmental conditions like humidity, smoke, wind, etc.

Many of these microphones provide multiple pickup patterns, selectable by a switch on the mic or, externally, on a remote control. Selecting different pickup patterns causes a change in electrical polarization; nothing is altered as far as the physical housing is concerned.

Creating Polar Patterns Electrically

Large diaphragm studio condenser mics with selectable patterns utilize a double-sided capsule with two moveable plates. The plates are charged with positive or negative polarity, in varying amounts, to shape virtually any polar response pattern. Some of these mics actually offer external control over polar response, which infinitely varies between patterns. The engineer, in the control room, shapes the microphone response to match the room and the source.

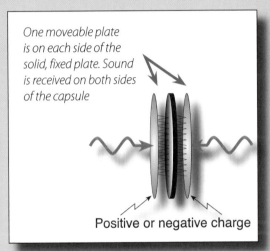

One moveable plate is on each side of the solid, fixed plate. Sound is received on both sides of the capsule

Positive or negative charge

Selectable Polar Patterns

Polarity requirements for each polar response pattern:

- Applying a positive charge to both moveable plates produces an omnidirectional response characteristic for the capsule.
- Applying a positive charge to one plate and a negative charge to the other, produces a bidirectional pattern.
- Varying the relative intensity of the charge between the two plates, as well as changing the backside plate from positive to negative, produces any variation or permutation of cardioid, bidirectional, and omnidirectional characteristics.

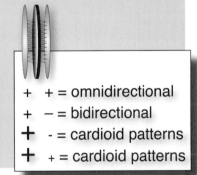

+ + = omnidirectional
+ − = bidirectional
+ - = cardioid patterns
+ + = cardioid patterns

These microphones achieve multiple directional characteristics by incorporating a double-sided capsule. This is merely an extension of the condenser capsule we discussed earlier; however, in this design there are two moveable plates, one on either side of the fixed backplate.

In this design, the microphone's directional characteristic is controlled through the application of varying amounts of positive and negative electrical charges to the two moveable plates:

- When both plates receive a positive charge, the mic exhibits omnidirectional characteristics.
- When the front plate receives a positive charge and the back receives a negative charge, the mic becomes bidirectional.
- As the intensity of the charging voltage varies between the two plates, the pickup pattern can be shaped at will, ranging from omnidirectional to bidirectional to cardioid, and on many mics multiple patterns in between. Most of these mics let the user select between preset pickup patterns through the use of a switch on the front of the mic. A few manufactures offer a remote control for pattern selection, some even offering a continuously variable balance of polarizing voltage. With this control, you can evaluate the sound in the control room, capturing the balance of the direct and ambient sound that make the most musical impact.

Video Example 5-2

Demonstration of Polar Pattern Changes

Some microphone designs actually incorporate two capsules to create directionality. An omnidirectional pickup pattern combined with a bidirectional pickup pattern produces a cardioid response.

The Proximity Effect

It's important to understand the *proximity effect*. The result of the proximity effect is this: As the microphone gets closer to its intended source, the low frequency range increases in relation to the high frequencies. It's not uncommon to see a rise of 20 dB at 100 Hz as the source gets close to the mic. Anyone who has used a handheld mic has probably recognized that, if they get closer to the microphone, the sound becomes bigger, louder, and more bass-heavy—this happens as a result of the proximity effect.

The proximity effect is most pronounced when using a microphone with a cardioid or bidirectional pickup pattern; it is least pronounced when using a microphone with an omnidirectional pickup pattern.

In effect, as a result of the proximity effect, the low frequency range increases in relation to the high frequency range. In reality, as the microphone moves closer to the source—a face, for instance—reflections from the source reflect back to the capsule out of phase, canceling more and more of the upper frequencies. The reflections not only cancel at the diaphragm, but they also enter through the ports, from behind the capsule and cancel. This explains why there is less of a problem with proximity effect when using a omnidirectional microphone—there's less cancellation because there are no ports.

Video Example 5-3

Demonstration of the Proximity Effect

Compensating for the Proximity Effect

To help compensate for the proximity effect, many microphones have a user-selectable highpass filter built in. When you're close-miking anything where the sound becomes to bass-heavy, simply apply the highpass filter. A typically highpass filter sets the cutoff frequency at 75 or 80 Hz. Some mics even let the user determine the cutoff frequency, typically offering various choices between 60 and 250 Hz.

Using the Proximity Effect to Our Advantage

The proximity effect isn't necessarily a bad characteristic of a microphone design, especially when we consider the effect it has on the close-miked sound in relation to the microphone's frequency response characteristic. Often, microphones with a unidirectional pickup characteristic exhibit a decreased sensitivity in the low frequencies, especially in a distant-miking application, and they're likely to exhibit an increased sensitivity in the high frequencies between 4 and 8 kHz.

Once we understand these tendencies, we realize that many microphones used in a close-miking application benefit from close proximity positioning. The increased low frequencies fill out an otherwise thin sound; and the extra sensitivity in the high-frequency range helps clean up the sound, resulting in greater understandability, presence, and clarity.

Response Characteristic

Frequency Response Curve

Almost any microphone responds to all frequencies we can hear plus frequencies above and below what we can hear. The human ear has a typical frequency response range of about 20 Hz to 20 kHz. Some folks have high-frequency hearing loss, so they might not hear sound waves all the way up to 20 kHz, and some small children might be able to hear sounds well above 20 kHz.

For a manufacturer to tell us that their microphone has a frequency range of 20 Hz to 20 kHz tells us absolutely nothing until they tell us how the mic responds throughout that frequency range. A mic might respond very well to 500 Hz, yet it might not respond very well at all to frequencies above about 10 kHz. If that were the case, the sound we captured to tape with that mic would be severely colored.

We use a *frequency response curve* to indicate exactly how a specific microphone responds to the frequencies across the audible spectrum.

The frequency response curve is the line on the graph that indicates the microphone's ability to reproduce frequencies across the audible spectrum. As the sensitivity to a frequency increases the curve ascends; as the sensitivity decreases the curve descends.

A microphone that is equally sensitive to all frequencies across the audible spectrum is represented by a flat-line curve on the 0 dB line—this is called a *flat* frequency response.

Frequency Response Curve

A mic with a flat frequency response adds very little coloration to the sound it picks up. Many condenser microphones have a flat, or nearly flat, frequency response. This characteristic, combined with the fact that they respond very well to transients, makes condenser mics very accurate.

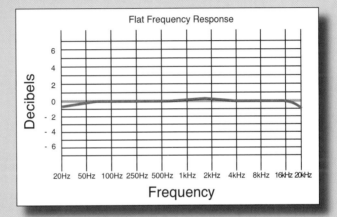

The mic represented by the curve below isn't very good at recording low-frequencies and it produces an abundance of signal at about 4 kHz. Though this mic wouldn't be very accurate, we could intelligently use a mic like this if we wanted to record a sound with a brutal presence. Many moving-coil microphones have this kind of frequency response curve. Moving closer to the mic helps fill out the low frequencies.

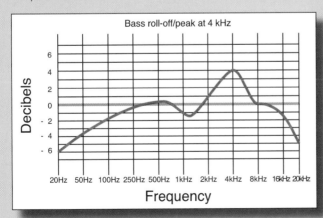

If a frequency response curve shows a peak at 5 kHz, we can expect that the mic will color the sound in the highs, likely producing a sound that has a little more aggressive sound than if a mic with a flat response was used. If the frequency response curve shows the low frequencies dropping off sharply below 300 Hz we can expect the mic to sound thin in the low end unless we move it close to the sound source to proportionally increase the lows.

A frequency response graph often contains more than one curve. The main, and typically more solid and bold curve, represents the on-axis frequency response. Other curves, on the graph, represent off-axis frequency response and, sometimes, comparisons between the responses in multiple sound fields.

Transient Response

The frequency response curve is one of the most valuable tools to help us predict how a mic will sound. What the frequency response curve doesn't tell us is how the mic responds to transients. We can predict the transient response of a mic based on what we already know about the basic operating principles of the different mic types. Therefore, condenser mics are expected to more accurately capture the fast transient, with moving-coil and ribbon mics lagging behind.

There is no real specification that quantifies a microphone's transient response. Ah! I guess there still is room for listening in this game of microphone choice!

Audio Example 5-3

Demonstration of Microphone Transient Response Characteristics

Output Characteristic

The output characteristic of a microphone quantifies factors like noise, sensitivity, overload limits, and impedance.

Equivalent Noise Rating/Self-Noise

A microphone's equivalent noise level, also referred to as *self-noise*, indicates the sound pressure level that will create the same voltage as the noise from the microphone.

Moving-coil and ribbon microphones are very quiet. They contain passive circuitry, which poses very little noise potential, and they have a very low self-noise.

A condenser microphones produces more self noise, simply because it contains amplifying circuitry necessary to boost the capsule signal up to mic level. The amplifying circuitry, though adding to the mic's self-noise, provides a hotter signal to the mixer; therefore, it needs less preamplification at the mixer input. So, there's a bit of a trade-off in terms of cumulative noise at the mixer output. There's slightly more mic noise and slightly less mixer noise.

Sensitivity

A microphone's sensitivity rating provides a way to compare microphone output levels. Sensitivity specifications are quantified as the microphone is given a specified frequency (typically 1 kHz) at a specified voltage. If two microphones receive the same acoustic signal, and one puts out more signal, it has a higher sensitivity rating.

Sensitivity ratings are sometimes expressed in dB, with the rating stated as a negative number: for example, −57 dB. This number quantifies the amount of boost required to amplifying the signal from the mic to line level—with line level at 0 dB.

When we compare microphone output in this way, we can identify mics with stronger output signals because their sensitivity is closer to zero. A microphone with a sensitivity rating of −35 dB has a much stronger output relative to a microphone with a sensitivity rating of −60 dB.

Sensitivity ratings are also expressed as a voltage comparison, in Volts/Pascal. Air pressure at the mic capsule is specified in Pascals and the resulting voltage from the microphone defines its sensitivity rating. If two microphones receive identical pressure (amplitude) and one puts out a higher voltage, that mic is said to have higher sensitivity. A Pascal is a standard pressure unit in the metric system, equal to one Newton per square meter—about 0.000145 pounds per square inch.

The only problem with sensitivity ratings is that manufacturers don't all use the same reference frequency or power rating. This specification is still useful in fundamental mic comparisons.

It is useful for us to compare the sensitivity ratings between moving-coil, ribbon, and condenser mics. When we compare apples to apples we find these comparisons to be true:

- Condenser microphones are typically the most sensitive, with ratings in the rage of −30 dB to −40 dB, or so.
- Moving-coil microphones are next in line with normal ratings in the −50 to −60 dB range.
- Ribbon microphones are often the least sensitive with ratings between −58 to −60, or so.

These comparisons are general and historically correct, considering classic microphone designs. Technology provides for extension of sensitivity in all the mic types. In fact, some of the modern ribbon mics actually receive phantom power in order to increase efficiency and to power an internal preamp much like the condenser mic.

Maximum SPL Rating

Most microphones can handle a lot of level (dB SPL) before they induce distortion. However, we sometimes need to mic loud instruments at close range, so distortion at the microphone can be an issue. It's important to be aware of the dB SPL where a specified percentage of distortion occurs (Total Harmonic Distortion). In addition, we need to realize the dB SPL, where the signal from the mic will clip, is the Maximum SPL rating referring to peak SPL. Keep in mind that the peak SPL rating is typically 20 dB greater than the average, or RMS, rating.

Moving-coil mics are capable of handling a bunch of level. They don't contain much other than the capsule and they're usually capable of handling peak SPL well in excess of 140 dB SPL peak, at acceptable distortion levels.

Condenser capsules are also capable of handling substantial level, however, the amplifying circuitry is likely to distort when subjected to loud sounds. Because of this, most condenser mics contain a pad, which decreases the signal strength from the mic capsule to its internal amplifying circuit (typically in 10 dB increments). Keep in mind that applying the pad diminishes the inherent signal-to-noise ratio by the amount of the pad; so implement it only when necessary.

Maximum SPL ratings always must be quantified at a specified total harmonic distortion (THD), and must be measure for the complete microphone (capsule and internal preamp). Most specification relate maximum SPL to .05% THD, though some reference 1% THD.

The distortion of a circular capsule doubles with each 6 dB increase in level, so it's a simple matter to calculate distortion ratings in relation to the published specification. If a microphone specifies 140 dB SPL peak at 0.5% THD, it's implied that the same microphone will exhibit 1% THD at 146 dB SPL peak, or .25% THD at 134 DB SPL peak.

Impedance

In the modern recording world microphones are low impedance devices. Most low-impedance mics fall in the impedance range between 50 and 250 ohms. High-impedance microphones are not common today; they were designed and optimized for use with vacuum tube amplification. High-impedance mics fall in the impedance range between 20,000 and 50,000 ohms.

Relating low-impedance ranges, mics with lower impedances, around 50 ohms, are more sensitive to electromagnetic hum and less susceptible to electrostatic interference, in relation to mics with impedances around 250 ohms. On the other hand, mics with impedances around 250 ohms are less sensitive to electromagnetic hum and more sensitive to electrostatic interference.

No matter what inherent noises mics with various impedance ratings are sensitive to, balanced low-impedance microphones are able to take advantage of the noise-canceling aspects of balanced circuitry; therefore, they benefit from the ability to run long cable lengths devoid of serious noise issues.

Conclusion

You can cover most home recording situations if you have at least one good moving-coil mic and one good condenser mic. With these two options available, you can fairly consistently achieve professional-sounding results.

This chapter was written with the intent to provide fundamental information that will immediately help you understand the practical applications of the three basic microphone types you use in the studio.

Dynamics Processors

It is fundamental to your recording success that you're completely familiar with the signal processing equipment. You need to recognize the sounds of these basic tools, and you need to know how to adjust their settings to fit each unique musical situation. It's surprisingly simple to learn the controls on most processors. Once you know how to use them, you possess knowledge that lets you operate similar units with minimal stress and maximum efficiency.

Each processor offers creative control and technical assistance. As we continue to build knowledge and skill, we'll see that each processor has many different and creative uses; and, try as we might, there are times when we find ourselves technically backed into a corner. In times like these, a thorough understanding of the right processor at the right time is very important.

According to my Funk & Wagnall's Standard Dictionary, *process*, when used as a verb, means to treat or prepare by a special method. A signal processor is doing just that to our music—treating and preparing it in order to form an appealing, appropriate, and intelligible blend of textures.

My thesaurus shows that synonyms for process are filter and sift. These, too, give an accurate image of what signal processors do. If we can filter our music like we can filter light, we can start with one color and end up with another. In the music and recording industry, musical textures are often referred to as colors.

Describing music and sounds verbally is a necessary skill. In the middle of a session, you will come up with some great ideas, and the more experienced you become, the more easily the ideas will flow. Your ideas are worthless if you can't verbalize them to the other musicians you're with. You don't need to use the most current jargon for a session to go well, but you must be sincere, proficient, and easy to get along with.

Notice that we consistently describe what we hear with terms normally used for things that we see, feel, or taste. Producers are notorious for using terms like dark, cold, bright, kickin', intense, sweet, etc. Describing the emotional impact of music involves describing far more than just what we hear. Good music is fundamentally a form of emotional expression and communicates to all feelings and senses. Be involved enough in your pursuits to walk the walk and talk the talk in a way that is sincere and easily understood.

Signal Processor Basics

A signal processor changes your musical signal for two basic reasons:

+ To enhance an existing sound
+ To compensate for an inherent problem with a sound

This section of The AudioMasters Series covers the three main categories of signal processors:

+ Dynamic range processors
+ Equalizers

* Effects processors (which include delays, reverberation, and multi-effects processors)

Communicating a Feeling

It's not always easy to communicate a subjective and artistic feeling with objective language. As you get better at producing great music, you'll need to be able to share your technical expectations effectively. The following list of descriptive terms, although common language, provide a starting point in the process of explaining your feelings in words that paint a visual picture on a sonic canvas.

As an example, you might recognize a signal that's been compressed with a 20:1 ratio, resulting in up to 20 dB of gain reduction with an extremely fast attack time of about 100 microseconds and a release time of 1.5 seconds or so, but until you can translate that to the word *squashed*, you are out of the musical communication loop.

Big: Containing a broad range of frequencies with ample clarity and sparkle in the highs and plenty of punch and thump in the lows. Usually contains large-sounding reverbs or large amounts of interesting reverb effects. Very impressive. Synonyms: huge, gigantic, large, monstrous.

Cool: The definition of cool changes with musical style. Very impressive, in a stylistically sophisticated way.

Dry: Without reverb or effect.

Edge: Upper frequencies of a sound that have a penetrating and potentially abrasive effect (typically 3 – 8 kHz). Used in moderation, these are the frequencies that add clarity and understandability.

Honk: See *squawk*.

Lush: Very smooth, pleasing texture. Often used in reference to strings that use wide voicings and interesting (although not extremely dissonant) harmonies. Typically includes a fair amount of reverb or concert hall.

Moo: Smooth, rich, and creamy lows.

Open: Uncompressed, natural, and clean with a wide dynamic range—

a sound that can be heard through, or seen through, to use a visual analogy. In a musical arrangement, a situation where there is a lot of space (places in the arrangement where silence is a key factor). Each part is important and audible, and the acoustical sound of the hall can be appreciated.

Raunchy: Often slightly distorted (especially in reference to a guitar). A sound that doesn't include the very high frequencies or the very low frequencies. Earthy and bluesy. When referring to musical style, indicates a loose and simple but soul wrenching performance.

Shimmer: Like sparkle in frequency content. Often includes a high frequency reverberation or some other type of lengthened decay.

Sizzle: See *sparkle*. Can also include the airy-sounding highs.

Sparkle: The upper frequencies of a sound. Includes the high bell-like sounds and upper cymbal frequencies from approximately 8 – 20 kHz. These are very high frequencies that add clarity and excitement.

Squawk: Midrange accentuation (approximately 1 kHz). Sounds a lot like a very small, cheap transistor radio.

Squashed: Heavily compressed. Put into a very narrow dynamic range.

Sweet: Similar to lush in that it is smooth and pleasing and includes a fair amount of reverb. Generally in a slightly higher register (above middle C). Pleasantly consonant.

Syrupy: Sweet, consonant sounds with ample reverberation. Often very musically and stylistically predictable.

Thump: Low frequencies. Especially, the lows that can be felt as well as heard (about 80 – 150 Hz).

Transparent: Nonintrusive. A sound that has a broad range of frequencies but doesn't cover all the other sound around it. A sound that silence can be heard through.

Verb: Reverberation.

Wash: Lots of reverb that runs from one note to the next. This is common on string pads, where the reverb becomes an interesting part of the pad texture. A producer will often ask the engineer to bathe the strings in reverb, so the engineer gives the producer a wash of reverb.

Wet: Reverberation. Doesn't include the direct, original sound. To say something is very wet indicates that it's heard with a lot of reverb and not too much of the original, non-reverberated sound. Sometimes used in reference to other effects as well.

Similarity of Hardware and Software Controls

In our study of signal processors, for now, there is little distinction between hardware and software plug-ins. The controls are typically identical and the intended effect is the same. In fact, it's very common for a software signal processor to mimic the sound and functionality of a classic piece of hardware.

Sonically, hardware and software processors are capable of providing excellent results; however, if they're used inappropriately, either will suck the life out of your recordings. Knowledge is the key; practice is the routine. There's not necessarily a right and wrong way to use signal processors, but there is a common and uncommon way. I aim to help you understand these valuable tools so that you can operate them efficiently, or if you want to paint outside the lines, you should at least do it intentionally.

Connecting Processors

Processors are typically connected to your system in one of only a few ways:

+ Channel inserts
+ Aux sends
+ Direct patch from instrument

Channel Insert

The channel insert on the mixer is an individual patch point on a channel. A piece of gear connected here becomes part of the signal from that point on. This patch point works very well for dynamic processors.

Aux Bus

For the most common and efficient way to incorporate an effects bus, plug the output of the aux bus into the input of the effects processor, then patch the output of the effects processor into an available channel or effects return. Always try to keep the effects return separate from the original dry track so that you can select the appropriate effect and balance for the final mix.

Use an aux bus to send the signal to the processor, and then return the affected sound to a mixer channel. This is the most flexible system for reverb and delay effects. In this way you can send multiple instruments, in varying levels, to one effects processor.

Plug the Instrument Directly into the Processor

It's also common, though not always efficient, to simply plug an instrument directly into the processor. The effectiveness of this technique depends on the application. In general, dynamic processors are used early in the recording process and at the beginning of the signal path, whereas effects processors are best reserved for mixdown.

Dynamics Processor Operation

Dynamic Range

Since these processors control dynamic range, this is an opportune time for a definition. *Dynamic range* is the distance, measured in dB, from the softest sound to the loudest sound. If an orchestra plays its loudest note at 115 dB and its softest note at 20 dB, its dynamic range is 95 dB—the loudest sound (115 dB) minus the softest sound (20 dB).

Dynamic range processors are often subtle in the effect they have on a musical sound, and in most situations, the listener shouldn't be aware that anything out of the ordinary is going on.

These processors (compressors, limiters, gates, and expanders) all work in a very similar way and have very similar, if not identical, controls from unit to unit. The task for any dynamic processor is to change the distance, in volume, from the softest sound to the loudest sound or to alter the dynamic range.

The VCA

The central operator in each of the dynamic processors is the VCA. VCA stands for *voltage-controlled amplifier*. Its name is almost its definition. Inside each processor is an amplifying circuit that turns up and down as it senses more or less voltage—it's a voltage-controlled amplifier. The changing levels in your musical signal determine the amount of voltage.

The VCA is capable of responding to increases or decreases in voltage by increasing or decreasing the output of the amplifying circuit. How it responds depends entirely on its intended function and the user adjustable parameters. Most dynamic range processors set the VCA so that, in relation to unity gain, it turns the signal level down in response to a specific voltage change, then turns back up again according to the parameter settings. However, there are a few applications where the VCA actually boosts the signal above its unity gain setting.

Keep in mind that software plug-ins, though they might digitally mimic the action of the VCA, still respond to level changes according to the user-adjusted settings in the same manner as hardware processors.

Dynamic range processors are typically patched into the signal path of the microphone, instrument, or recorder track via the channel insert

Patching the Dynamic Processor

Dynamic processors are typically inserted into a channel. The output of the processor, when patched into the channel return, supplies the dynamically altered signal back into the channel signal path—it's a permanent part of the sound from that point.

It's also common to patch a source directly into a dynamics processor before it reaches the mixer.

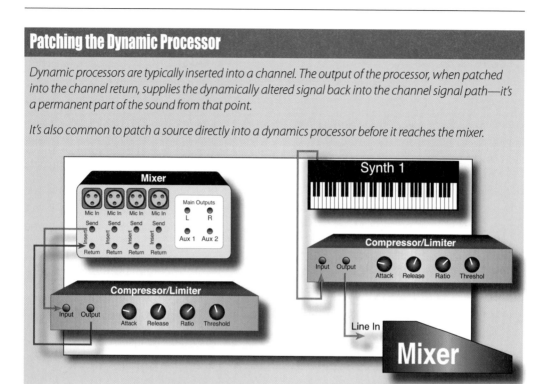

(on the mixer or the patch bay). They're also commonly patched inline between the source and the mixer.

Substitutes for the VCA

The VCA (Voltage-Controlled Amplifier) is an analog amplifier, which is controlled by variations in voltage. This is the primary dynamic control circuit in most compressors, limiters, gates, and expanders.

There are options to the VCA—they include

* The DCA (Digitally-Controlled Amplifier) is an analog amplifier, which is controlled by variations in digital data. Some of the most highly regarded consoles combine the warmth and purity of analog circuitry with the precision and flexibility of digital control. In addition to precision, digital control data is easily stored, automated, and recalled.

+ The Optical Level Control offers a very smooth and precise level control system utilizing a light-dependent resistor called an opto-isolator. When light shines on this special resistor some of the signal is shunted to ground, which reduces the level. Processor parameters are dependent on reactions to light intensity.

+ Data Control operates in the digital domain to control dynamics through mathematical calculations. The actions of the VCA or DCA are simulated according to digitally encoded instructions. As long as the algorithms are well founded, digital manipulation is very accurate and efficient.

Although there are multiple possible device that control the dynamic processor level, we'll typically refer to the VCA generically as the controller.

Compressor/Limiter

The compressor is an automatic volume control that turns loud parts of the musical signal down. When the VCA senses the signal exceeding a certain level, it acts on that signal and turns it down.

Imagine yourself listening to the mix and every time the vocal track starts to get too loud and read too hot on the meter, you turn the fader down and then back up again for the rest of the track. That is exactly how a compressor works.

A compressor is a useful tool when recording instruments with a wide dynamic range. Compressors are typically used on vocals, bass, or any other instruments with a wide dynamic range.

Again, the VCA in a compressor only turns down in response to a signal and then turns back up again; it doesn't turn up beyond unity gain (the original level.)

Why Do We Need a Compressor?

We need a compressor to protect against overly loud sounds that can overdrive electronic circuitry, oversaturate magnetic tape, or overdrive digital or analog inputs. A compressor also helps even out the different ranges of an instrument. Instruments like brass, strings, vocals and guitars can have substantially different volumes and impact in different pitch ranges. These ranges can disappear, then suddenly jump out in a mix. A highly skilled and very focused engineer might catch many of these variations in level, but a compressor is often more reliable and less intrusive. A compressor can also even out volume differences created by an artist changing their distance from the mic.

The Resulting Effect of Compression

Since we've put a lid on the loud passages and can therefore print the entire track, with a stronger signal, to the recorder. We are able to move the overall signal into a tighter dynamic range, which is especially useful in a commercial popular genre that's often played on radio or television. This gives us a better signal-to-noise ratio.

When used correctly, compression doesn't detract from the life of the original sound. In fact, it can be the one tool that helps that life and depth to be heard and understood in a mix. Imagine a vocal track. Singers perform many nuances and licks that define their individual style. Within the same second, they may jump from a subtle, emotional phrase to a screaming-loud, needle-pegging, engineer-torturing high note. Even the best of us aren't fast enough to catch all of these changes by simply riding the input fader. In this situation, a compressor is needed to protect against excessive levels.

This automatic level control gives us a very important by-product. As the loudest parts of the track are turned down, we're able to bring the overall level of the track up. In effect, this brings the softer sounds up in relation to the louder sounds. The subtle nuance becomes more noticeable in a mix, so the individuality and style of the artist is more easily recognized, plus the understandability and audibility of the lyrics are greatly increased.

The End Result of Compression

Ideally, the end result of compression is that the loudest portion of the signal sound about the same as normal, but the softest portions seem louder.

A compressor automatically turns the loud parts down as soon as it senses their levels. Once the signal passes the user-set threshold, the VCA acts on the signal according to the ratio setting.

This graph represents the compression of the wave above. Everything below the threshold is unaffected. Everything above the threshold is reduced in level according to the ratio setting.

The pink line represents the level of the compressed signal above. Once the compressor has turned the loudest part of the track down, the entire track can be turned up so the overall level still reaches 0 VU. The red line represents the new level. Notice that the softest parts of the track are louder (consequently easier to hear in the mix) as the entire level increases.

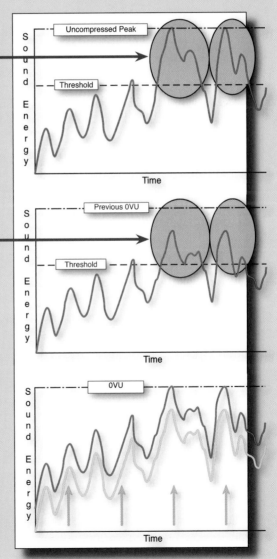

Analog versus Digital Application

If you're using analog tape, compression is very important during tracking. Since the noise floor is so high when using magnetic tape, the best way to keep your recordings free from tape noise is to compress the tracks into a relatively tight dynamic range and record the hottest level possible to tape. In effect, this brings the softer sounds up further away from the noise floor; so, if they need to be turned up in the mix, they're as clean and noise-free as possible.

However, application of compression during mixdown, when you're using an analog multitrack, increases the likelihood that the noise level will audibly raise and lower during the mix. As the compressor rides the level of important tracks, like the lead or backing vocals, the airy hiss (called tape noise) tends to turn up during the softer more open portion, and then it disappears during the loud and complex sections. When the VCA turns the tape track back up during the soft passages, the tape noise is audibly increased, too. We hear this noise turning up and down as the signal crosses the threshold, and the VCA reacts by turning up and down. This is one of the adverse effects of compression. The sound of the noise turning up and down is called *pumping* or *breathing*.

In the digital realm, noise is not really the issue, but there are still a few good reasons to use compression when tracking or mixing.

- First, in a commercial mix, each ingredient is carefully placed, so, whether digital or analog, compression helps define the position and focus of a track.
- Second, whether a vocal or instrumental track, compression helps increase the relative level of the nuance, resulting in increased understandability and impact.

✦ Third, in the digital realm bit depth equates to amplitude resolution, so it's important to record full digital levels at some point to insure maximum definition. Compression helps us to record at higher digital levels with less concern about exceeding maximum level and achieving clipping or digital distortion.

To Compress, or Not to Compress—That Is the Question

Some engineers use a lot of compression and limiting; other engineers don't us any. In commercial popular music, the use (and over use) of dynamic processors is common. Most engineers want their mixes to sound the loudest, in relation to other commercial mixes—it becomes an obsession for most. Therefore, each ingredient is tightly placed in its own dynamic, pan, and frequency range. Then the entire mix is limited so it's as loud as technically possible.

The only problem with compression obsession is that, in an effort to create a mix that's big and loud, the result can be narrow and lifeless, especially when there are a lot of mix ingredients. Good production, great music, and excellent recording technique is the real keys to a big sound.

Many producers and engineers don't like the sound of the compressor working. They prefer the natural space around a pure sound, and they rarely incorporate compression in tracking or mixdown. However, though they don't use automatic dynamic processors, they typically ride the levels of the tracks as they're being recorded or mixed—in effect, they're acting as human, real-time compressors.

It's common for engineers to use dynamics processors very conservatively during tracking, adjusting compression for minimal gain reduction, then assessing the need for further compression during mixdown. This technique is much more realistic in the digital realm.

You need to assess the viability of using compression for each instance during the recording process. Evaluate the music, the intended audience, the musicians, the genre, and your own personal taste. There are a lot of cases where I, personally, like the sound of a track or song that's been compressed. Other times I like a more natural sound. Also, just because you're using a compressor, doesn't mean you have to overuse it.

Compression Parameters

There are five controls common to most compressors: threshold, attack time, release time, ratio, and output level.

Once you see how these work, you can operate any compressor, anywhere, anytime. To make it even better, these controls are easy to understand, and they do just what they say they do.

Threshold

As amplitude increases, voltage increases. The threshold is the point where the compressor begins to recognize the signal amplitude. Once the compressor recognizes the signal—when the amplitude rises above a certain voltage—it begins to act in a way that is determined by the attack time, release time, and ratio controls.

There are two different ways that compressors deal with the threshold:

+   One way boosts the signal up into the threshold. Picture yourself in a room with an opening in the ceiling directly overhead. You represent the signal, with your head being the loudest sounds. The opening represents the threshold of the compressor. Imagine that the floor moves up and you begin to go through the opening. That's the way that some compressors move the signal into the threshold—they turn it up until it goes through the threshold.

◆ The other way compressors deal with the threshold is by moving it down into the signal. Picture yourself in a room with an opening directly overhead. Now the ceiling moves down until you're through the opening. This is the other way the threshold control works—the signal level stays the same but the threshold moves down into the peaks.

No matter which way the threshold works, it's the part of the signal that exceeds the threshold that's processed. Once the signal is through the threshold, the VCA turns down just the part of the signal that's gone through, leaving the rest of the signal unaffected. The portion that's above the threshold will be turned down according to how you have set the remaining controls (attack time, release time, and ratio).

Controls on the Compressor/Limiter

Almost all compressor/limiters contain the same control options, whether hardware or software. Once you understand the functions on one compressor/limiter, you'll find seamless transition to another. The unit pictured here contains the basic controls: attack time, release time, threshold, ratio, output level, Peak/RMS, Knee, and meter function.

The Moving Threshold

The threshold control moves the threshold up or down in relation to the energy of the signal. Anything above the threshold is acted on by the VCA. Anything below the threshold is left unaffected.

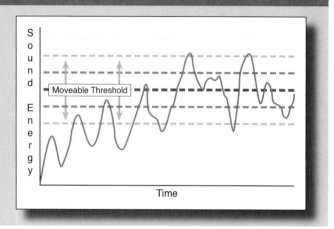

Attack Time

The attack time controls the amount of time it takes the compressor to turn the signal down, once it's passed the threshold. If the attack time is too fast, the compressor will turn down the transients. This can cause an instrument to lose life and clarity. On a vocal, for instance, if the attack time is too fast, all of the "t" and "s" sounds will start to disappear. On the other hand, if the attack time is too slow and the vocal is very compressed, the Ts and Ss will fly through uncompressed and sound exaggerated.

Audio Example 6-1

Ss and Ts

Audio Example 6-2

Exaggerated Ss and Ts

Variations in the attack time setting helps diminish or accentuate the relative attack of instruments like guitar, bass, piano, or drums. Long attack times adjust average levels; short attack times adjust peak levels.

Specific attack time limitations vary between processors, though they typically range from 0.1 ms to 200 ms. One characteristic of an expensive compressor is fast attack time capability. Also, some compressors have the attack time fixed for a specific purpose, like vocals.

Using the Attack Time Setting to Control Understandability and Punch.

The Attack setting provides a means to adjust the relative level of the initial portion of an audio source. In a vocal passage, the initial transient sounds—especially the sounds "s," "t," and "k"—offer two possible complications for recording:

1. If the vocalist has a natural abundance of sibilance, the recorded track might take on a harsh character. These transient sounds, called sibilance, can cause distortion of analog tape, irritating effects when reverberated, and they can even overdrive electronic circuitry. In this case, a fast attack time, during compression, helps smooth out the sound—the track will settle into the mix better.

2. If the instrumental bed is very percussive, and if the vocal sound contains understated sibilance, the lyrics might be lost in the mix because they're not understandable. In this case, try compressing the vocal track, using a slower attack time; the compressor will let the sibilance pass through unaltered, yet the rest of the word will be compressed according to the control settings. The length of attack time varies with each vocal sound and application, but settings between 5 and 50 ms typically work well. Listen to the sound as you make the attack time adjustment; once you find the right setting, the vocal will seem more alive and understandable.

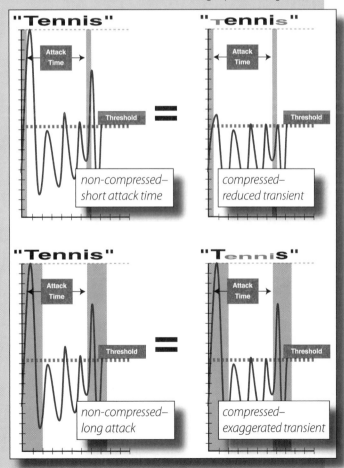

Release Time

Release time is the time that it takes for the compressor to let go, or turn the signal back up, once it's below the threshold. The release time might be as fast as 50 ms or as slow five seconds.

Fast release times work well with fast attack times to control peak levels. Slow release times work well with slow attack times to control average levels. There is no practical value to adjusting the attack time so it's slower than the release time.

Long release times with severe compression can result in increased sustain. With the proper setting of the threshold, release, and attack time, a guitar, for example, can benefit by increased sustain. Over time, as the VCA turns the signal back up to its original level, an otherwise quickly decaying signal maintains its sustain longer.

For a natural and unobtrusive sound, set the release time relatively fast and the release time relatively slow. Each instrument or voice is different, so there's still importance placed on listening while you adjust these controls.

Ratio

Once the compressor starts acting on the signal, the *ratio* control determines how extreme the VCA action will be. The ratio is simply a comparison between the level that goes through the threshold and the output of the VCA; it's expressed as a mathematical ratio (10:1, 3:1, etc.). The first number, in the ratio, indicates how many dB of input increase will result in 1 dB of output increase. The higher the ratio, the greater the compression.

If the threshold is adjusted so that the loudest note of the song exceeds the threshold by 3 dB, and the ratio is 3:1, the 3 dB peak is reduced to a 1 dB peak—the gain is reduced by 2 dB. Using that same

3:1 ratio, if you input a 12 dB peak, the unit would output a 4 dB peak—still a ratio of 3:1 and a gain is reduced by 8 dB.

Output Level

The output level control makes up for reduction in gain caused by the VCA. If the gain has been reduced by 6 dB, for example, the output level control is used to boost the signal back up to its original level.

Compression with a 3:1 Ratio

The threshold in the top graph is set so that the peak sound energy level exceeds the threshold by 12 dB. The VCA turns the signal (above the threshold) down according to the ratio. With the ratio set at 3:1, the VCA only allows 1 dB of increase for every 3 dB that exceed the threshold. The original signal exceeded the threshold by 12 dB (with no compression), but the compressor only allows a 4 dB peak when the ratio is set at 3:1 (bottom graph).

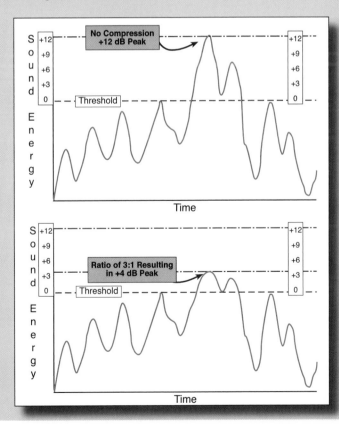

The Difference Between a Compressor and a Limiter

It's the ratio setting that determines the difference between a compressor and a limiter. Ratio settings below 10:1 result in compression. Ratio setting above 10:1 results in limiting. That explains why most manufacturers offer combined compressor/limiters. Extreme compression becomes limiting.

Hard Knee versus Soft Knee Compression/Limiting

Hard Knee/Soft Knee selection determines how the compressor reacts to the signal once it passes this threshold and the amplifier circuitry engages. Whereas the ratio control determines the severity of compression, the knee determines how severely and immediately the compressor acts on that signal.

When the compressor is set on soft knee and the signal exceeds the threshold, the amplitude is gradually reduced throughout the first 5 dB, or so, of gain reduction. When the compressor is set on hard knee and the signal exceeds the threshold, it is rapidly and severely reduced in amplitude. The Hard Knee/Soft Knee settings are still dependent on the ratio, attack, release, and threshold settings. The knee setting specifically relates to how the amplifier circuitry reacts at the onset of compression or limiting.

The difference between hard knee and soft knee compression is more apparent at extreme compression ratios and gain reduction. Soft knee compression is most useful during high-ratio compression or limiting. The gentle approach of the soft knee setting is least obvious as the compressor begins gain reduction. Hard knee settings are very efficient when extreme and immediate limiting is called for, especially when used on audio containing an abundance of transient peaks.

Typically, soft knee compression is more gentle and less audible than hard knee. Try this setting on a lead vocal or lyrical instrument for inconspicuous level control.

Hard knee dynamic control is more extreme and much less sonically forgiving. Try hard knee limiting when absolute level control is necessary.

Peak/RMS Detection

RMS refers to average signal amplitude, based on the mathematical function of the Root Mean Square. Peak refers to immediate and transient amplitude levels, which occur frequently throughout most audio

Hard Knee versus Soft Knee Compression/Limiting

Once the compressor senses signal above the threshold and the attack time has passed, the level-control circuitry begins to respond. A hard knee setting activates the dynamic process immediately; a soft knee setting gradually engages dynamic control during the first 5 dB, or so. Typically, soft knee compression is more gentle and less audible than hard knee —try this setting on a lead vocal or lyrical instrument for inconspicuous level control.

Hard knee dynamic control is more extreme and much less sonically forgiving. Try hard knee limiting when absolute level control is necessary.

The dynamic action matches the word picture—soft knee creates a gently rounded level adjustment; hard knee creates a sharp angle.

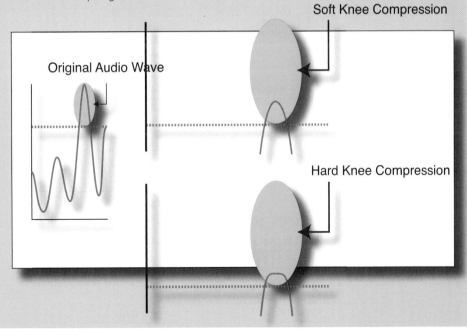

recordings. The Peak/RMS setting determines whether the compressor/limiter responds to average amplitude changes or peak amplitude changes. RMS compression is more gentle and in obtrusive than peak compression. Peak compression is well suited to limiting applications. It responds quickly and efficiently to incoming amplitude changes containing transient information.

Side Chain

The side chain provides an avenue for activating the level-control circuitry from a source other than the audio signal running the unit.

Any audio source can be patched into the side chain input for creative applications. However, it's common to run a split from the audio signal through an equalizer then back into the side chain. In this way, the equalizer can be boosted at a specific frequency and cut at others, allowing the user to select a problem frequency to trigger gain reduction. This technique works very well when low frequency pops or thumps must be compressed while the rest of the audio signal is left unaffected, or when certain high-frequency transients must be controlled.

Listen to the following audio examples highlighting the sonic impact of different compressor/limiter settings. The acoustic guitar is often compressed, and in these examples it provides an excellent comparison. With its clean, clear sound and transient attack, the parameter adjustments are very apparent.

Audio Example 6-3

Acoustic Guitar – No Compression

This acoustic guitar, recorded without compression, has clean sound, however, it has a wide dynamic range. Notice the difference between the level of the loudest sound and the softest sound.

Side Chain Control of the Level-Changing Circuitry

Use the side chain send and return to control dynamics from an external source. This illustration demonstrates a common use for side chain inserts during compression or limiting.

Notice the analog inputs and outputs are connected in the normal manner—the actual audio signal does not pass through the equalizer. The side chain send routes the audio to the equalizer, then the signal is equalized to accentuate an problem frequency.

Once it has been equalized, the signal is patched back into the unit through the side chain return. When the side chain circuit is enabled, the compressor's level detection circuit reacts to the equalized signal instead of the regular analog input.

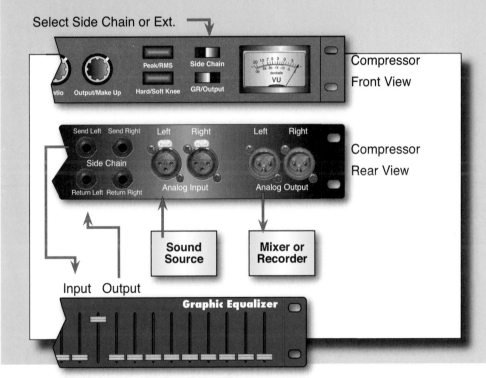

Audio Example 6-4

Acoustic Guitar – Variations in Attack Time Settings

Notice the change in the attack of each note. By increasing and decreasing the attack time, intimacy and sonic impact change dramatically.

Audio Example 6-5

Acoustic Guitar – Long and Short Release Times

With the release time set too short, the processor is continually active, risking sonic degradation. With the release time set too short, the level changes become very noticeable.

Audio Example 6-6

Acoustic Guitar – Ratios: From Compression to Limiting

Each ratio setting provides a different result, from gentle gain control to the brick wall.

Audio Example 6-7

Acoustic Guitar – Adjusting the Threshold for Optimum Sonics

Listen to the changing sound as the threshold move down into the signal amplitude. If the threshold is too high, there is no dynamic compression. If the threshold includes too much of the amplitude, the level-changing circuitry (VCA, DCA, Optical Am, etc.) is always working; this typically produces a thin, weak, or strained sound.

Audio Example 6-8

Acoustic Guitar – Adjusting the Knee and Peak/RMS Settings

With the ratio set at 7:1, attack time at 10 ms, release time at .5 seconds, and the threshold set for 6 dB of gain reduction, notice the sonic difference as I switch from soft to hard knee, and from Peak to RMS detection.

Meters on the Compressor/Limiter

Compressor/limiters utilize various systems for metering gain reduction, input levels, and output levels. Some devices offer separate meters for each function; whereas, several units utilize a multipurpose meter that switches between functions. Either system is functionally simple, and it's important to use these meters to help insure optimal use of the device.

Input Level Meter

Ideally, the input level meter verifies the proper signal strength as it enters the device; however, many compressor/limiters don't have one. Since compressor/limiters are usually patched inline directly or through an insert, you can take advantage of the meters on your mixer.

When the compressor limiter is in bypass mode (most units have a bypass switch) the output is likely at unity gain with the output, when the output level is set to "U" or zero (no boost or no cut). Therefore, as you increase gain reduction, you should be able to simply boost the output level to maintain the original level or, if your device doesn't have an output level control, you can usually make the gain up by increasing the channel gain trim.

Output Level Meter

The output level meter is simply fed by the output level control. Use it to verify that the signal level is correct at the output of the device. It's common to set the output level so that it matches the input level—both at unity gain.

Gain Reduction Meter

Gain reduction refers to the amount that the VCA has turned the signal down once it crosses the threshold.

To meter gain reduction, some compressor/limiters use a series of LEDs and others use a VU meter. Typically, LEDs light up from right to left, indicating how far the unit has turned the signal down. Each LED represents two or more dB of gain reduction.

If your compressor has a VU meter, 0 VU is the normal (rest) position on a meter used to indicate no gain reduction. As the compressor turns down, the needle moves backwards from 0 to indicate

VU Meter versus LEDs versus Onscreen

Each dynamic processor provides a method to measure the amount of gain reduction occurring at any given time. Whereas, a typical meter reads from left to right, to indicate the amount of signal present, a compressor/limiter meter typically moves from right to left to indicate the amount of signal decrease (in dB).

When a traditional VU meter indicates gain reduction, there is no level change as long as the meter is resting at the far right side. As the level is decreased, the meter moves to the left—the numbers on the meter represent decibels of gain reduction.

When a series of LEDs are used to indicate gain reduction, each LED that illuminates indicates more gain reduction. The numbers under each LED show the amount of gain reduction.

Computer-based compressor/limiters use an onscreen version of either of these metering systems.

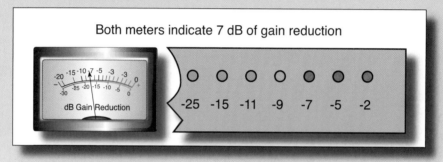

Both meters indicate 7 dB of gain reduction

the amount of gain reduction. A −5 reading on the VU indicates 5 dB of gain reduction.

Video Example 6-2

Same Source Through Different Compressor/Limiter Settings

The Function of a Compressor

The goal of the compressor is to gently ride the signal level in the same way that a human engineer would ride the fader while listening to the track playback. In most cases, the listener shouldn't even realize there's a processor being used.

Technical Effect

Technically speaking, a compressor allows the engineer to record an entire track at a hotter level than if the compressor were not included. If the compressor decreases the level of the hottest part of the track by a 6 dB, the entire track can be recorded 6 dB hotter—making up the reduced gain—without over modulating, saturating the tape, or exceeding the maximum digital recording level. Since the compressor should be transparent and seamless as it controls the maximum output level, the result is a more visible, audible, and apparent audio track, especially during the passages containing the least amplitude. In other words, the loud passages should exhibit minimal sonic effect, while the soft passages should be louder than they'd have been without the compressor. Though the compressor/limiter actually controls the loudest passages, the net result for the listener is an increase in the level of the softer passages.

Audio Example 6-9

Vocal Compressed by 6 dB

Listen to this example of a vocal phrase: first, the original non-compressed recording, then the same phrase compressed by 6 dB.

Musical Effect

Musically speaking, the compressor is very useful. The lead vocal track, for example, should be audible, understandable, and apparent throughout most popular commercial songs; this is precisely the result of compression. A compressed lead vocal track typically sounds more up front in the mix; it remains within its intended dynamic range.

Bass guitar is nearly always compressed. The low-frequency range of the bass contains an abundance of energy; therefore, it produces an abundance of amplitude. Left unchecked, this abundance of low-frequency energy can dominate the overall mix level. For example, when the bass part is particularly strong the overall mix level might be artificially hot. When the bass is properly compressed, however, that energy is kept in check, the bass remains consistently supportive of the mix, and the mix level can be increased.

Any instrument with a wide dynamic range can benefit from compression. However, certain classical and orchestral recordists use little or no compression. The natural dynamic range of the orchestra, piano, symphony, or instrumentalist adds emotional impact and reality to the recording. Many of these recordings are listened to in an environment conducive to such dynamic range: a living room, family room, media room, or listening space designed specifically for the enjoyment of music. In these instances, the natural dynamic range can be appreciated. On the other hand, many commercial popular recordings are listened to in a car, grocery store, mall, or other high ambient noise environments. Any dynamic subtleties might be lost when listened to in these places, so it's important that all the mix ingredients reside within the audible audio spectrum. Therefore, compression is very appropriate for these recordings.

The Function of a Limiter

A limiter and compressor perform the same basic task, although, a compressor controls level and amplitude in a soft and gentle manner, while a limiter controls level and amplitude in an extreme way. The choice to use compression or limiting is purely a musical one. For example, when recording a bass guitarist with a very consistent playing style, there might be little need for compression. However, if the same bassist slaps or snaps during a particular take, a limiter could help level out the amplitude peaks caused by these aggressive musical instances.

Limiters are often used to control the level of an entire mix. An excellent mix typically contains several transient peaks (levels that exceed the average level of the entire mix). Although the limiter ignores the majority of the program material (audio that doesn't exceed the threshold), a peak which exceeds the threshold will be turned down quickly. Through the use of limiters, most commercial recordings maintain a constant and aggressive level and amplitude. A master mix might peak at 0 VU; while the limited mix also peeks at 0 VU, the only difference is that the limited mix sounds louder. A good limiter operates in a way that is imperceptible to most listeners. It reacts quickly to transient peaks and maintains a full, impressive, aggressive sound throughout the limiting process.

Limiting

This graph represents a signal with a huge peak energy. Use a limiter on this kind of signal so the majority of the sound is unaffected (by the limiter's VCA) but the trouble spot is nearly eliminated.

The limiter can keep nearly any peak from overdriving the tape or from blasting through the mix. The results of effective limiting are often dramatic. If you start with a mix that has been level-impaired by a few quick blasts of energy, then you essentially remove those blasts, the entire mix level can be increased substantially, resulting in a much more powerful sound.

The limiter has reduced a huge peak (nearly 100 dB) to a peak of approximately 1 dB.

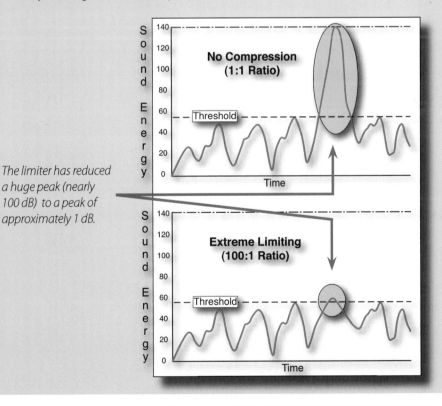

Meters Compared During Limiting

This video segment demonstrates the limiting of a complete mix. The meter on the left shows the output level of the non-limited audio. The meter on the right shows the output of the same audio, limited by 6 dB.

Making Up Gain That's Been Reduced

Now listen to the difference in volume between the two mixes, once the limited mix is boosted 6 dB to make up the gain reduction.

Proper Use of the Compressor/Limiter

Typically, the threshold is set above normal operating levels—most of the time, there should be no gain reduction. If there's always gain reduction, the VCA is always working, and you begin to lose the clarity and signal integrity. An experienced engineer tries to eliminate unnecessary amplifying circuits in the signal path—that's our approach here. The VCA should only act when it's needed.

Compressors and limiters are generally used while recording tracks as opposed to during mixdown, since one of the main benefits in compressing the signal is that you can get a more consistently hot signal on tape.

Listen to the different versions of the exact same vocal performance in Audio Examples 6-11 to 6-15. I've adjusted the level so that the peak of each version is at the same level. The only difference is the amount of compression. Pay special attention to the understandability of each word, the apparent tape noise, and the overall feel of each track.

Audio Example 6-11

No Compression

Audio Example 6-12

3 dB Gain Reduction

Audio Example 6-13

6 dB Gain Reduction

Audio Example 6-14

9 dB Gain Reduction

Audio Example 6-15 includes tape noise with the vocal. Listen to the compressor turning up and down (pumping and breathing).

Audio Example 6-15

Pumping and Breathing

Should I Use the Compressor/Limiter on Input or Output?

The compressor/limiter is typically used at the beginning of the signal path, just after the source enters the mixer input; however, there are valid reasons to incorporate this tool at each stage of the signal path. Compression and limiting provide an efficient means of controlling the level that's recorded to tape, hard disk, or any other analog or digital media. Recording instruments with a wide dynamic range often require constant level adjustments to insure a consistently acceptable signal-to-noise ratio. These level changes can be performed manually, although they're typically much more reliable when performed electronically.

It's common to compress or re-compress audio tracks or groups during mixdown. Compressing the lead vocal or a stereo group of backing vocals during mixdown provides the engineer the opportunity to finely craft their positioning within the dynamic audio spectrum. However, avoid over-compressing any signal. Part of the power of audio rests in its dynamic content. When robbed of dynamic contrast, music and other audio sources lose impact. A mix devoid of dynamic contrast is tedious to for the listener. Music is, at its very essence, a balance of tension and release. Sound that remains constant in amplitude and energy provides no release and eventually wears the listener out. Strive to find the best dynamic contrast for your music.

Setup Suggestions for the Compressor/Limiter

+ Adjust Ratio to determine function. Setting below 10:1 produce compression; setting 10:1 to infinity:1 produce limiting.
+ Set attack time fast or slow, depending on the audio source and desired effect
+ Set release time to about .5 seconds for general use.
+ Select Soft Knee for gentle compression, or Hard Knee for limiting applications
+ Select RMS for most compression applications, or Peak for most limiting applications.
+ Adjust the threshold for the desired amount of gain reduction.
+ Adjust the threshold for the amount of gain reduction that you want. You should typically have 3 – 6 dB of reduction at the strongest part of the track, and there should be times when there is no gain reduction.
+ Consider all rules carefully, then break them at will, and intentionally, anytime the music demands.

This is the text book approach for the most natural and least audibly conspicuous compression.

If you've achieved 6 dB of gain reduction, you're able to boost your overall level to tape by 6 dB over what it would have been without the compressor. With the entire track boosted, we can hear the nuances and softer passages more clearly. As an additional bonus, the complete track (including the soft passages) will be 6 dB further away from the noise floor than they were before compression, or the bit resolution will be increased.

Compressors are essential tools for making professional sounding audio recordings. If you are involved in audio for video and television, compressors are essential because of the limited dynamic range in these mediums.

How Much Is Enough?

Though the musical and artistic needs of any recording must dictate the use and application of all available tools, there are some guidelines for most tasks which should be considered.

Compression and limiting are generally most effective when gain reduction occurs several times throughout a recording, yet most of the audio is left untouched—beneath the threshold. If the compressor/limiter is always turning the signal down and back up again, optimum gain reduction is not being achieved; in addition, adverse side effects called pumping and breathing occur.

Pumping

Pumping is the result of the level-control circuitry reducing gain, as the amplitude exceeds the threshold, then turning it back up again as the signal dips below the threshold. In some very "in-your-face" commercial pop music, a certain degree of pumping is acceptable to some artists; however, there are other ways to keep the mix optimally present without risking serious audio quality degradation. Pumping is often viewed as more extreme than breathing.

Breathing

Breathing is like pumping, although the actual breathing sound is derived from a signal with a high noise content. As the noise, or room ambience, is decreased and increased as it crosses the threshold, it creates a sound similar to breathing. Whereas pumping and breathing are essentially the same technical anomaly, pumping is often associated with a full range signal, and breathing is associated with an airy, high-frequency sound.

Audio Example 6-16

More Pumping and Breathing

Listen to these example of pumping and breathing. Notice the difference in the effect as the audio content changes.

Commercial Pop Music

Commercial pop music is often highly compressed and limited. The fact that most highly commercial music is heard in listening environments with intrusive ambience motivates artists and producers to contain their recording an a very narrow dynamic range—the music must be heard over road noise, crowd noise, clanking glasses, breaking plates, and the "blue-light special" announcement. Most commercial recordings head immediately up to 0 VU and stay there through the duration of the song; this doesn't make for a very emotionally dynamic work of art, but it does produce music that consistently holds the listener's attention.

Classical Recording

Classical recordists typically use compression and limiting sparingly. The dynamic realism of a symphony or soloist—held in high regard throughout the classical listening community—is very integral to artistic expression. Too much dynamic processing changes the balance between ambience and music, altering the individualism of a highly-skilled ensemble or artist.

When included, dynamic processing is typically very subtle and understated. Limiting is sometimes used for extreme peaks, or gentle compression might be included to help smooth out the loudest sections; however, dynamic processing is almost always subtle and sonically inconspicuous.

The Purist and Compression

The audio purist always strives to eliminate amplifying circuitry from the signal path. Therefore, many engineers prefer to control levels manually, using a mixer fader, to facilitate the most accurate, pristine, and natural-sounding recording. However, compressors and limiters have been so commonly used in commercial music recording that the sound achieved by their use has become expected; the impact, dynamic control, and punch that they provide has become, in some producer/engineer's opinions, sonically essential.

Multiband Compressor/Limiters

Dynamic processing of a full-bandwidth signal presents a unique set of considerations. A single instrument or voice is typically functional in a specific frequency range; extreme bandwidth isn't a real consideration. In these instances, a full-bandwidth compressor/limiter is effective and preferred. On the other hand, a full-bandwidth recording (like a complete mix of a commercial pop song) contains an impressive amount of all frequencies. Low-frequency content contains the greatest amplitude, so, when running this type of signal through a full-range compressor/limiter, the low frequencies tend to activate the gain reduction circuitry first and most often. As the mix level changes in response to the bass frequencies, the high frequencies also change; they decrease during gain reduction, then they increase as the signal is turned back up.

Audio Example 6-17

Full-Range Recording Through a Normal Compressor

Listen to this example of a full-range recording passing through a normal compressor/limiter. Notice how the high frequencies ride along with the lows, as gain reduction comes and goes.

A multiband compressor/limiter divides the audio into multiple frequency ranges (frequency bands). Each frequency band is compressed separately. Whereas the audible spectrum is typically divided into lows, mids, and highs, the actual crossover points, between bands, is often user-adjustable. Since each frequency range is dynamically controlled independent of the others, there is less audible pumping and breathing, and the mix stays more consistently in the forefront of the dynamic spectrum.

Most commercial mixes pass through some form of multiband compression, eventually. Mastering engineers use these tools to help raise the overall level and impact of recordings so they'll sound loud and full in comparison with other professional recordings. Overuse of the multiband compressor can result in a lifeless sound; On the other hand, tastefully aggressive multiband dynamic control can result in a very punchy and impressive recording.

Listen to this example of a full-bandwidth mix passing through a multiband compressor/limiter. Notice the change in sound as the processor switches in and out.

Be aware that, as the bands compress separately, the mix changes slightly. When the low-frequency gain is reduced, the highs and mids will probably stick out more in the mix; or, when the mids are reduced the vocals might be suddenly buried. Careful selection of ratios and crossover points between bands will usually solve these problems, though these details do require your utmost attention.

Audio Example 6-18

Full-Range Recording Through a Multiband Compressor

De-Essers

A de-esser is a frequency specific compressor, which reacts quickly to signals with strong high-frequency content—in particular, the common frequency range of the letters "s," "t," and "k." The purpose of the de-esser is to compensate for poorly compressed vocals. When a vocal track is recorded with the threshold too low and the attack time too slow, the initial transient sounds are overexaggerated, resulting in over-modulation of analog tape, over-stimulation of reverberation, and just a generally obnoxiously sibilant sound. Since the de-esser reacts quickly to high frequencies, it can usually solve a sibilance problem.

Multiband Compressor/Limiters

Multiband compression divides the audible spectrum into multiple bands, compressing each band separately. This typically provides a very punchy and powerful sound, although it offers the most potential for coloration as each band responds uniquely.

The WAVES L3 multiband limiter, below, provides separate limiting for five user-selected bands. In addition, tools like these often provide level adjustment for each band, giving the user a chance to influence overall timbre.

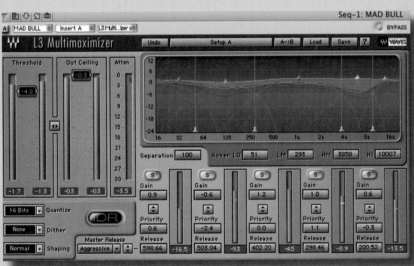

Most compressor/limiters can function as a de-esser. Simply select a fast attack time, patch the side chain to an external equalizer which has the frequencies between about 3 and 6 kHz boosted (depending on the sound being de-essed), select the side chain as the processor trigger, then adjust the threshold so gain reduction occurs whenever a transient problem occurs.

Tube versus Solid-State Compressor/Limiters

Compressor/limiters, throughout the years, have been manufactured using vacuum tube circuitry, solid-state circuitry, and even a combination of both. Some engineers just love old equipment: They love the look, they love the history, they love the feel, and they love the sound. Realistically, high-quality compressors and limiters are very useful, whether they use tube or solid-state technology. Listen to the tool, then choose the sound that provides the best support for the musical vision.

Tube technology typically sounds warmer and fuller than solid-state technology, especially as it's pushed to the limit of its capability. When a vacuum-tube audio circuit reaches distortion the waveform is smoother and more rounded than a comparable solid-state waveform. In comparison, distortion of a solid-state circuit causes the waveform to be clipped off in an extreme way, creating a harsh and brittle sound. For this reason, musical styles that contain a wide dynamic range, or very aggressive instrumentation and orchestration, are often recorded using tube technology.

Listen to the difference in the sound between these compressors. Keep in mind that these are tools; tubes might be the best for one application while solid-state is better for another.

Solid-state technology is, in theory, far quieter than tube technology. Utilizing high-quality solid-state compressor/limiters is very desirable in a context where the amplifying circuitry is not being over taxed. They can be the most accurate and sonically purer compressors and limiters, as long as the processor has plenty of headroom to avoid any kind of waveform distortion.

Audio Example 6-19

Sonic Comparison of Tube and Solid-State Compression

The Gate/Expander

The gate and expander are in the same family as the compressor/limiter. They're also centered on a VCA, and the VCA still turns the signal down. When the VCA is all the way up, the signal is at the same level as if the VCA weren't in the circuit—unity gain.

When the compressor/limiter senses the signal passing the threshold in an upward way, it turns down the signal that's above the threshold. The amount of gain reduction is determined by the ratio control. In contrast, when the gate/expander senses the signal passing the threshold in a downward way, the VCA turns the signal down even further. In other words, everything that's below the threshold is turned down.

The Controls on a Gate/Expander

The controls on the gate/expander are essentially the same as the controls on a compressor/limiter. The threshold is the control that determines how much of the signal is acted on by the unit. The attack and release times do the same thing here that they did on the compressor: They control how quickly the unit acts once the signal has passed the threshold and how fast the unit turns the signal back up once the signal is no longer below the threshold.

The range control on the expander/gate correlates to the ratio control on the compressor/limiter. In fact, some multifunction dynamic processors use the same knob to control both ratio and range. The ratio on a compressor determines how far the VCA turns the signal down once it passes the threshold in an upward direction. The range on a gate/expander determines how far down the VCA will turn the signal once it passes the threshold in a downward direction.

When the signal gets below the threshold and the range setting tells the VCA to turn all the way off, the unit is called a *gate*. When the signal is below the threshold, the gate is closed. The gate closes behind the sound and doesn't open again until the signal is above the threshold.

The range can also be adjusted so that the VCA only turns down the signal part of the way once it gets below the threshold. In this case, the unit is called an *expander*.

The Gate/Expander

Anything above the threshold is unaffected by the gate/expander's VCA. The gate/expander turns anything below the threshold down or off.

Notice the portions of the sound wave that have been turned down by the VCA. Anything below the threshold can be effectively silenced.

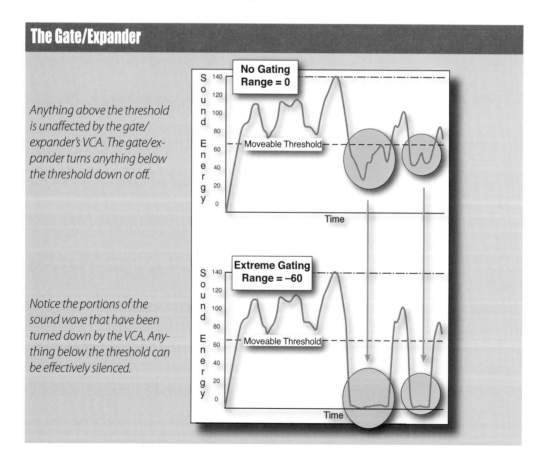

A gate is called a gate because it opens and closes when it senses the signal come and go across the threshold. An expander is called an expander because it expands the dynamic range of the music. It creates a bigger difference between the softer and the louder sound by turning the softer parts down.

The most common type of expander doesn't turn the louder parts up; it just seems to in relation to the softer parts. Specifically, an expander that turns the softer sounds down is called a *downward expander*. There is also an upward expander, which boosts the louder parts above unity. Upward expanders aren't very common and are somewhat noisy and difficult to control in a medium such as magnetic tape. Unless I specify otherwise, I'll refer to a downward expander throughout this course simply as an expander.

Gates versus Expanders

Gates are especially useful in getting rid of noise, either from an instrument like a noisy electric guitar or from tape. If the threshold is set just above the noise floor, as the signal fades to the noise, the gate will simply continue the fade to silence. An expander can do exactly the same thing, but it will turn the noise down rather than off. Gates and expanders can really clean up a recording by getting rid of noise between the musical segments of each track.

Some units have a separate button to select the gate or the expander. Both the gate and the expander have the same controls, including full use of the range control. I've found that expanders are usually smoother in their level changes and are typically more musical and glitch free than gates.

Expanders are useful for restoring dynamic range to a signal that has been severely compressed. If the compressor reduced the loud parts by 9 dB, then, in theory, if the signal is expanded and the range control is adjusted to turn the soft parts down by 9 dB, we should have a pretty reasonable facsimile of our original dynamic range.

Gates and expanders are usually used on mixdown, rather than when recording tracks. If the gate or expander threshold were set incorrectly, some softer notes might not get printed to tape because they couldn't open the gate. If this happens, these softer notes are gone forever. Thus, the safest approach is to use gates and expanders on mixdown. During mixdown, the threshold can be non-destructively adjusted.

In a small setup, we often need to gate as we're recording (if we're going to gate at all) because of a lack of tracks and gates. This can work just fine, but more care must be taken in setting the processor, and the musical performance must be more consistent and predictable. For instance, a noisy guitar track is often gated during recording because the noise is consistent and it's easy to set the threshold so that the guitar sound comes through fine and the noise never touches tape.

So, a gate and an expander are really the same tool. The gate is an extreme version of an expander, with the gate turning the soft parts off where the expander just turns them down.

Audio Example 6-20
Guitar – No Gate

Audio Example 6-21
Guitar – Gated

Audio Example 6-22
Hi-Hat – No Expander

These dynamic range processors are all very useful, and often essential, in creating professional sounds. Each unit offers many creative and musical possibilities. As we study the individual instruments and their unique sound schemes, we'll use these processors time and again.

The Digital Realm and Gates

With the advent of digital workstations and computer-based audio software packages, gates have become less useful on mixdown. Although a gate is still a useful tool to assist in getting rid of noise like that from a guitar processor, digital control of track levels during mixdown has become a simple matter, and it's dependable and fast.

Effects Processors

Effects processors add the third dimension to a mix. Room size and complexity is indicated by the way sound reacts in an acoustical space. The echoes and delays that happen after the original sound emanates from the source tell the brain what the surrounding environment is like. All of the effects processors (echoes, reverberation, and chorus effects) revolve around one thing: the delay.

Wet versus Dry

Wet and *dry* are two terms that refer to the amount of effected signal that is blended with the original dry signal. The relation ship between wet and dry is quantified in a percentage; 100% wet refers to a signal that contains none of the original (dry) signal. A sound that is completely dry has none of the effect return combine with it (0% wet). An equal combination of the wet and dry signals is referred to as 50% wet.

Patching Effects Devices

It's best to connect the output of your mixer's aux bus or effects send bus to the input of the effects unit. Next, connect the output of the effect to the mixer's effects return or into an available mixer channel.

Most effects processors have a meter on the input for proper level adjustment, and many effects processors have a final output level adjustment.

When using effects it's always desirable to keep the original track dry and blend the 100% wet return with it for the best musical impact.

Patching Effects Processors

It's best to connect the output of your mixer's aux bus or effects send bus to the input of the effects unit. Next, connect the output of the effect to the mixer's effects return or into an available mixer channel.

When using effects, keep the original track dry, blending the 100% wet return with it for the best musical impact.

In a small setup you might have to run the effects in-line, doing all of the blending from dry to wet within the effects unit. This can work well, but it's best to keep the dry and wet controls separate.

Delay Effects

A delay does just what its name says: It hears a sound and then waits for a while before it reproduces it. Current delays are simply digital recorders that digitally record the incoming signal, and then play it back with a time delay selected by the user. Delay parameters vary from unit to unit, but most delays have a range of delay length from a portion of a millisecond up to one or more seconds. This is called the delay time or delay length and is typically variable in increments of a millisecond.

Almost all digital delays are much more than simple echo units. Within the delay are all of the controls you need to produce slapback, repeating echo, doubling, chorusing, flanging, phase shifting, some primitive reverb sounds, and any hybrid variation you can dream up.

Slapback Delay

The simplest form of delay is called a slapback. The slapback delay is a single repeat of the signal. Its delay time is anything above about 35 ms. Any single repeat with a delay time of less than 35 ms is called a double.

To achieve a slapback from a delay, simply adjust the delay time and turn the delayed signal up, either on the return channel or on the mix control within the delay.

For a single slapback delay, feedback and modulation are set to their off positions. Slapback delays of between 150 ms and about 300 ms are very effective and common for creating a big vocal or guitar sound.

Audio Example 7-1 demonstrates a track with a 250 ms slapback delay.

Audio Example 7-1

250 ms Slapback

Slapback delays between 35 and 75 ms are very effective for thickening a vocal or instrumental sound.

Audio Example 7-2 demonstrates a track with a 50 ms delay.

Audio Example 7-2

50 ms Slapback

Slapback delay can be turned into a repeating delay. This smooths out the sound of a track even more and is accomplished through the use of the regeneration control. This is also called feedback or repeat.

This control takes the delayed signal and feeds it back into the input of the delay unit, so we hear the original, the delay, and then a delay of the delayed signal. The higher you turn the feedback up, the more times the delay is repeated. Practically speaking, anything past about three repeats gets too muddy and does more musical harm than good.

The vocal track in Audio Example 7-3 starts with a simple single slapback, then the feedback raises until we hear three or four repeats.

Audio Example 7-3

Repeating Delays

Why does a simple delay make a track sound so much bigger and better? Delay gives the brain the perception of listening in a larger, more interesting environment. As the delays combine with the original sound, the harmonics of each part combine in interesting ways. Any pitch discrepancies are averaged out as the delay combines with the original signal. If a note was sharp or flat, it's hidden when heard along with the

Calculating Delay Times

Delays are an important part of creating a professional-sounding mix. It's usually best if the delays are in time with the music—it helps reinforce the groove.

Calculating the delay time per beat is simple, especially if you're recording to a Digital Audio Workstation, using the built-in sequencer as a click. Use this formula: 60,000 ÷ bpm to find the length of one beat. Here's the logic. If you keep it tucked away in your memory banks, you'll never need to look at a sheet of numbers in a grid again.

- *There are 1000 ms/second*
- *There are 60 seconds/minute*
- *Therefore, there are 60,000 ms/minute.*
- *Tempos are stated in beats per minute (bpm)*
- *Therefore, the total number of ms/minute (60,000) divided by the number of beats in a minute derives the number of ms per beat.*

There are typically four beats per minute. Delays that work well, in support of the musical groove, are in time with the quarter note, eighth note, sixteenth note, or eighth- and sixteenth-note triplets.

To calculate these subdivisions of the beat, divide the ms/beat

- *By 1.5 to calculate the quarter note triplet value.*
- *By 2 to calculate the eighth note value.*
- *By 3 to calculate the eighth note triplet value.*
- *By 4 to calculate the sixteenth note value.*
- *By 6 to calculate the sixteenth note triplet value.*

delay of a previous note that was in tune. This helps most vocal sounds tremendously and adds to the richness and fullness of the mix.

The human brain gets its cue for room size from the initial reflections, or repeats, that it hears off surrounding surfaces. Longer delay times indicate, to the brain, that the room is larger. The slapback is really perceived as the reflection off the back wall of the room or auditorium as the sound bounces back (slaps back) to the performer. Many great lead vocal tracks have used a simple slapback delay as the primary or only effect. Frequently, this delay sounds cleaner than reverb and has less of a tendency to intrusively accumulate.

Slapback delay, often called *echo*, is typically related in some way to the beat and tempo of the song. The delay is often in time with the eighth note or sixteenth note, but it's also common to hear a slapback in time with the quarter note or some triplet subdivision. The delay time affects the rhythmic feel of the song. A delay that's in time with the eighth note can really smooth out the groove of the song, or if the delay time is shortened or lengthened just slightly, the groove may feel more aggressive or relaxed. Experiment with slight changes in delay time.

It's easy to find the delay, in milliseconds, for the quarter note in your song, especially when you're working from a sequence and the tempo is already available on screen. Simply divide 60,000 by the tempo of your song (in beats per minute). 60,000 ÷ bpm = delay time per quarter note in milliseconds (in Common time).

The slapback effect is often smoothed out by regenerating the delay, essentially creating multiple echoes or repeats. It's common to use a delay with two to five, or more, delays. This has a blending affect on most mixes.

Doubling/Tripling

Combining a single delay of less than 35 ms with the original track is called *doubling*. Combining two separate delays of less than 35 ms with the original track is called *tripling*. The short delay(s) can combine with the original track to sound like two people (or instruments) on the same part. Often, performers will actually record the same part two or three times to achieve the doubled or tripled sound, but sometimes the electronic simulation is quicker, easier and sounds more precise. Audio Example 7-4 demonstrates an 11 ms delay (with no feedback and no modulation) combined with the original vocal. At the end of the example, the original and the delayed double pan apart in the stereo spectrum. This can be a great sound in stereo, but is a potential problem when summing to mono.

When doubling, use prime numbers for delay times. You'll hear better results when your song is played in mono. A prime number can only be divided by one and itself (e.g., 1, 3, 5, 7, 11, 13, 17, 19, 23, 29 and so on).

Modulation

The modulation control on a delay is for creating chorusing, flanging and phase shifting effects. The key factor here is the LFO (low frequency oscillator); its function is to continually vary the delay time. The LFO is usually capable of varying the delay from the setting indicated by the delay time to half of that value and back. Sometimes the LFO control is labeled modulation.

As the LFO is slowing down and speeding up the delay, it's speeding up and slowing down the playback of the delayed signal. In other words, modulation actually lowers and raises the pitch in exactly the same way that a tape recorder does if the speed is lowered and raised. Audio Example 7-5 demonstrates the sound of the LFO varying the delay time. This example starts subtly, with the variation from the original going down slightly, then back up. Finally, the LFO varies dramatically downward, then back up again.

On most usable effects, these changes in pitch are slight and still within the boundaries of acceptable intonation, so they aren't making the instrument sound out of tune. In fact, the slight pitch change can have the effect of smoothing out any pitch problems on a track.

As the pitch is raised and lowered, the sound waves are shortened and lengthened. When know that two waveforms follow the same path, they sum together. The result is twice the amount of energy. We also know that when two waveforms are out of phase, they work against and cancel each other, either totally or partially.

When the modulation is lengthening and shortening the waveform and the resulting sound is combined with the original signal, the two waveforms continually react together in a changing phase relationship. They sum and cancel at varying frequencies. The interaction between the original sound and the modulated delay can simulate the sound we hear when several different instrumentalists or vocalists perform together. Even though each member of a choir tries their hardest to stay in tune and together rhythmically, they're continually varying pitch and timing. These variations are like the interaction of the modulated delay with the original track. The chorus setting on an effects processor is simulating the sound of a real choir by combining the original signal with the modulated signal.

The speed control adjusts how fast the pitch raises and lowers. These changes might happen very slowly, taking a few seconds to complete one cycle of raising and lower the pitch, or they might happen quickly, raising and lowering the pitch several times per second.

Audio Example 7-6 demonstrates the extreme settings of speed and depth. It's obvious when the speed and depth controls are changed here. Sounds like these aren't normally used, but when we're using a chorus, flanger, or phase shifter, this is exactly what is happening, in moderation.

Audio Example 7-6

Extreme Speed and Depth

Phase Shifter

Now that we're seeing what all these controls do, it's time to use them all together. Obviously, the delay time is the key player in determining the way that the depth and speed react. If the delay time is very, very short, in the neighborhood of 1 ms or so, the depth control will produce no pitch change. When the original and affected sounds are combined, we hear a distinct sweep that sounds more like an EQ frequency sweeping the mids and highs. With these short delay times, we're really simulating waveforms, moving in and out of phase, unlike the larger changes of singers varying in pitch and timing. The phase shifter is the most subtle, sweeping effect, and it often produces a swooshing sound.

Audio Example 7-7 demonstrates the sound of a phase shifter.

Audio Example 7-7

Phase Shifter

Flanger

A flanger has a sound similar to the phase shifter, except it has more variation and color. The primary delay setting on a flanger is typically about 20 ms. The LFO varies the delay from near 0 ms to 20 ms and back, continually. Adjust the speed to your own taste.

Flangers and phase shifters work very well on guitars and Rhodes-type keyboard sounds. They provide a rich blend and interesting harmonic motion.

Audio Example 7-8 demonstrates the sound of a flanger.

Audio Example 7-8

Flanger

Chorus

The factor that differentiates a chorus from the other delay effects is, again, the delay time. The typical delay time for a chorus is about 15 to 35 ms, with the LFO and speed set for the richest effect for the particular instrument voice or song. With these longer delay times, as the LFO varies, we actually hear a slight pitch change. The longer delays also create more of a difference in attack time. This also enhances the chorus effect. Since the chorus gets its name from the fact that it's simulating the pitch and time variation that exist within a choir, it might seem obvious that a chorus works great on background vocals. It does. Chorus is also an excellent effect for guitar and keyboard sounds.

Audio Example 7-9 demonstrates the sound of a chorus.

Audio Example 7-9

Chorus

Phase Reversal and Regeneration

The regeneration control can give us multiple repeats by feeding the delay back into the input so that it can be delayed again. This control can also be used on the phase shifter, chorus and flange. Regeneration, also called feedback, can make the effect more extreme or give the music a sci-fi feel. As you practice creating these effects with your equipment, experiment with feedback to find your own sounds.

Most units have a phase reversal switch that inverts the phase of the affected signal. Inverting the phase of the delay can cause very extreme effects when combined with the original signal (especially on phase shifter and flanger effects). This can make your music sound like it's turning inside out.

Audio Example 7-10 starts with the flanger in phase. Notice what happens to the sound as the phase of the effect is inverted.

Audio Example 7-10

Inverting Phase

Stereo Effects

The majority of effects processors are stereo, and with a stereo unit, different delay times can be assigned to the left and the right sides. If you are creating a stereo chorus, simply set one side to a delay time between 15 and 35 ms, then set the other side to a different delay time, between 15 and 35 ms. All of the rest of the controls are adjusted in the same way as a mono chorus. The returns from the processor can then be panned apart in the mix for a very wide and extreme effect. Listen as the chorus in Audio Example 7-11 pans from mono to stereo.

Audio Example 7-11

Stereo Chorus

For a stereo phase and flange, use the same procedure. Simply select different delay times for the left and right sides.

Delay Settings for Various Delay Effects

Effect	Delay A	Delay B (Stereo)	LFO	Speed	Regeneration	Phase
Slapback	35–350ms		No	No	No	No
Echo (Repeats)	35–350ms		No	No	2–10	No
Reverb	15-35ms	15-35ms	No	No	Several	No
Doubling	1-35ms		No	No	No	No
Tripling	1-35ms	1-35 ms	No	No	No	No
Phase Shifter	0.5-2ms	0.5-2 ms	Yes	Low	Medium	Yes/No
Flanger	10-20ms	10-20ms	Yes	Low	Medium	Yes/No

Understanding what is happening within a delay is important when you're trying to shape sounds for your music.

Sometimes it's easiest to bake a cake by simply pressing the Bake Me a Cake button, but if you are really trying to create a meal that flows together perfectly, you might need to adjust the recipe for the cake. That's what we need to do when building a song, mix or arrangement; we must be able to custom fit the ingredients.

Reverberation Effects

As we move from the delay effects into the reverb effects, we must first realize that reverb is just a series of delays. In fact, modern reverberation devices are capable of all delay effects. However, some devices are limited to producing either delay or reverberation effects. Also, many software plugins specifically focus on a single function, often in emulation of classic hardware.

Reverberation is simulation of sound in an acoustical environment, like a concert hall, gymnasium or bedroom. No two rooms sound exactly alike. Sound bounces back from all the surfaces in a room to the listener or the microphone. These bounces are called reflections. The combination of the direct and reflected sound in a room creates a distinct tonal character for each acoustical environment. Each one of the reflections in a room is like a single delay from a digital delay. When it bounces around the room, we get the effect of regeneration. When we take a single short delay and regenerate it many times, we're creating the basics of reverberation.

Reverb must have many delays and regenerations working together in the proper balance, combining to create a smooth and appealing room sound.

Envision thousands of delays bouncing (reflecting) off thousands of surfaces in a room and then back to you, the listener—that's what's happening in the reverberation of a concert hall or any acoustical environment. There are so many reflections happening in such a complex order that we can no longer distinguish individual echoes.

Accurate and believable digital simulation is accomplished by producing enough delays and echoes to imitate the smooth sound of

Slapback Delay and Reflections

Sound travels at the rate of about 1120 ft./sec. To calculate the amount of time (in seconds) it takes for sound to travel a specific distance, divide the distance (in feet) by 1120 (ft./sec.): time = distance (ft.) ÷ speed (1120 ft./sec.).

In a 100' long room, sound takes about 89 ms to get from one end to the other (100÷1120). A microphone at one end of this room wouldn't pick up the slapback until it completed a round trip (about 178 ms after the original sound).

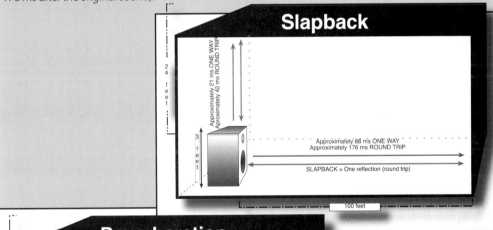

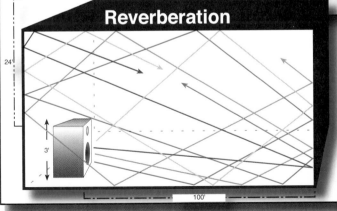

natural reverb in a room. The reason different reverb settings sound unique is because of the different combinations of delays and regenerations. The mathematic calculation and relations of the delays involve in a reverberation sound is call an *algorithm*.

A digital reverb is capable of imitating a lot of different acoustical environments and can do so with amazing clarity and accuracy. The many different echoes and repeats produce a rich and full sound. Digital reverbs can also shape many special effects that would never occur acoustically. In fact, these sounds can be so fun to listen to that it's hard not to overuse reverb.

Keep in mind that sound perception is not just two dimensional, left and right. Sound perception is at least three dimensional, with the third dimension being depth (distance). Depth is created by the use of delays and reverb. If a sound (or a mix) has too much reverb, it loses the feeling of closeness or intimacy and sounds like it's at the far end of a gymnasium. Use enough effect to achieve the desired results, but don't overuse effects.

Most digital reverberation devices offer several different sounds. These are usually labeled with descriptive names like halls, plates, chambers, rooms, etc.

Hall Reverb

Hall indicates a concert hall sound. These are the smoothest and richest of the reverb settings, with complex, long delay times that blend together to form a smooth decay over time. Typical hall algorithms have a decay time longer than 2 seconds, although user-adjustable controls allow for unnatural settings on hall sounds or any of the basic sounds.

Chamber Reverb

Chambers imitate the sound of an acoustical reverberation chamber, sometimes called an echo chamber. Acoustical chambers are fairly large rooms with hard surfaces. Music is played into the room through high-quality, large speakers, and then a microphone in the chamber is patched into a channel of the mixer as an effects return. Chambers aren't very common now that technology is giving us great sounds without taking up so much real estate. The sound of a chamber is smooth, like the hall's, but has a few more mids and highs.

Plate Reverb

Plates are the brightest sounding of the reverbs. These sounds imitate a physical plate reverb. A true plate is a large sheet of metal (about 4' by 8') suspended in a box and allowed to vibrate freely. A speaker attached to the plate itself induces sound onto the plate. Two contact microphones are typically mounted on the plate at different locations to provide a stereo return. The sound of a true plate reverb has lots of highs and is very clean and transparent.

Room Reverb

A room setting imitates many different types of rooms that are typically smaller than hall or chamber sounds. These can range from a bedroom to a large conference room or a small bathroom with lots of towels to a large bathroom with lots of tile.

Rooms with lots of soft surfaces have little high-frequency content in their reverberation. Rooms with lots of hard surfaces have lots of high-frequency content in their reverberation.

Reverse Reverb

Most modern reverbs include reverse or inverse reverb. These are simply backwards reverb. After the original sound is heard, the reverb swells and stops. It is turned around. These can actually be fairly effective if used in the appropriate context.

Gated Reverb

Gated reverbs have a sound that is very intense for a period of time, and then closes off quickly. They offer a very big sound without overwhelming the mix.

Though, at one time this was a trendy, popular sound, the technique has been around for a long time. The original gated reverb sound actually used a room mic, distant from the source, in a large room patched through a gate. The trigger for the gate to open was set to the side chain, where a mic close to the source was patched. This was common on snare drum at one time. There was a close mic on the snare patched to the mixer and also patched into the trigger input of the gate, so when the snare was hit, the gate opened and you could hear the large sound of the room microphone(s). When the snare wasn't being hit the room mics were off.

Other Variations of Reverberation

There are many permutations of the reverberation sounds. You might see bright halls, rich plates, dark plates, large rooms, small rooms, or bright phone booth, but they can all be traced back to the basic sounds of halls, chambers, plates, and rooms.

These sounds often have adjustable parameters. They let us shape the sounds to our music so that we can use the technology as completely as possible to enhance the artistic vision. We need to consider these variables so that we can customize and shape the effects.

Audio Example 7-12

Reverberation Variations

Video Example 7-1

Various Acoustic Space Recordings

Effects Parameters

Predelay

Predelay is a time delay that happens before the reverb is heard. This can be a substantial time delay (up to a second or two) or just a few milliseconds. The track is heard clean (dry) first, so the listener gets

Diffusion

Reverberation with low diffusion often sounds grainy because the reflections that make up the reverb sound are relatively far apart. There are some reverberation algorithms that sound good with lower diffusion, especially in the context of an up tempo musical work. Low diffusion reverb sounds don't usually work well in a very open ballad.

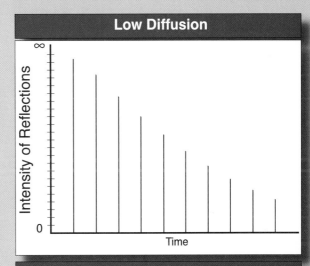

High diffusion usually results in a smooth-sounding reverb. Since the reflections are close together in time, they blend together to create a wash of reverberation. If the arrangement or orchestration is very busy and the reverberation has high diffusion, the mix might sound too thick. High diffusion works well on ballads and very exposed arrangements.

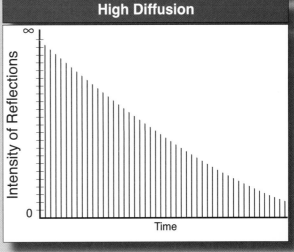

more of an up-front and close feel, then the reverb comes along shortly thereafter to fill in the holes and add richness.

Diffusion

Diffusion controls the space between the reflections. A low diffusion is equated with a very grainy photograph. We might even hear individual repeats in the reverb. A high diffusion is equated with a very fine grain photograph, and the sound provides a very smooth wash of reverb.

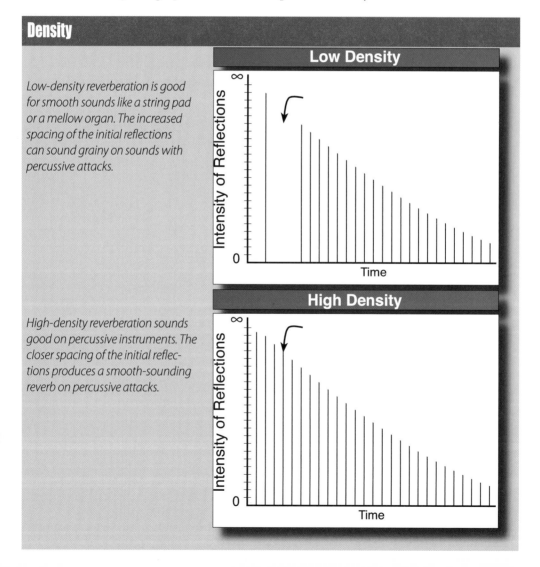

Density

Low-density reverberation is good for smooth sounds like a string pad or a mellow organ. The increased spacing of the initial reflections can sound grainy on sounds with percussive attacks.

High-density reverberation sounds good on percussive instruments. The closer spacing of the initial reflections produces a smooth-sounding reverb on percussive attacks.

Decay Time

Reverberation time, reverb time and decay time all refer to the same thing. Traditionally, reverberation time is defined as the time it takes for the sound to decrease to one-millionth of its original sound pressure level. In other words, it's the time it takes for the reverb to go away.

Decay time can typically be adjusted from about 1/10 of a second up to about 99 seconds. We have ample control over the reverberation time.

Density

The density control adjusts the initial short delay times. Low density is good for smooth sounds like strings or organ. High density works best on percussive sound.

Audio Example 7-13

Reverberation Parameters

Effects Plug-Ins

There are so many options, when it comes to effects plug-ins! The key, at this point, is that you understand the effects parameters and the sonic impact they have. The parameters are the same, across the board, whether you're recording with hardware or software. The nice thing about software plugins is that they typically have infinite control over every imaginable parameter. There is nothing between you and your creative options. That fact that there is an attractive visual interface for each software plug-in also aids in the understanding of how the effects are created, altered, and used.

Summary

In the recording world of yesteryear the only way to adjust reverberation time was to dampen or undampen the springs in the spring reverb tanks or physically move a bar that moved a felt pad onto, or off of, the plate reverb. Trying to control reverb time in a true reverberation chamber is even more difficult. Current technology provides a myriad of variables when shaping reverb sounds. In fact, when you consider the number of possible options, it is mind boggling. We can design unnatural hybrids like a large room with a very short decay time and plenty of high frequency, or any other natural or unnatural effect.

Each parameter is important, and as we deal with individual guitar, drum, keyboard, and vocal sounds, reverb is a primary consideration.

Modern-day multi-effects processors typically sound great and offer countless control options. When you're selecting any device that provides reverberation effects, listen to it before you buy it. Some manufacturers really have the algorithms that sound great; other manufacturers wish they did.

Don't overlook the classic devices. They still sound good and provide unique creative options that are waiting to be rediscovered.

Index